HOW TO MAKE
MONEY
ON THE
INTERNET

This is a **FLAME TREE** book
First published in 2012

Publisher and Creative Director: Nick Wells
Senior Project Editor: Catherine Taylor
Copy Editor: Anna Groves
Art Director: Mike Spender
Layout Design: Jane Ashley and Mike Spender
Screengrabs: Rob Hawkins
Digital Design and Production: Chris Herbert
Picture Research: Rob Hawkins, Caitlin O'Connell and Catherine Taylor
Proofreader: Kenneth Emmanuel
Indexer: Helen Snaith

Special thanks to: Caitlin O'Connell

12 14 16 15 13
1 3 5 7 9 10 8 6 4 2

This edition first published 2012 by
FLAME TREE PUBLISHING
Crabtree Hall, Crabtree Lane
Fulham, London SW6 6TY
United Kingdom
www.flametreepublishing.com

Flame Tree Publishing is part of Flame Tree Publishing Ltd

ISBN 978-0-85775-390-8

Printed in China

All images courtesy Rob Hawkins and © Flame Tree Publishing, except the following which are courtesy Shutterstock.com and
© the following contributors: Tischenko Irina 1t & 3t; Robbi 1b & 70; Vicente Barcelo Varona 3b & 106; wrangler 4& 16; Kenneth V.
Pilon 5b & 92; Minerva Studio 5t & 52; Doreen Salcher 6b & 150; Pavel Ignatov 6t & 120; EmiliaU 7b & 228; Yuri Arcurs 7t & 212, 165;
pressureUA 8; wrangler 9; auremar 10 & 253, 98, 110, 122cl, 136tr; iodrakon 15; trekandshoot 18; Edw 21br; Korn 21l; Jo Lomark 26;
Brian A Jackson 27; Zadorozhnyi Viktor 30, 77; Kaspri 31; Kaspars Grinvalds 33; Elena Elisseeva 35; Paul McKinnon 45; chungking 47;
IngridHS 54; Kurhan 58; Kuzma 62; Kzenon 69; Lee Torrens 71; Plus69 75; McIek 84; Jirsak 85, 141; Terri Francis 90; caimacanul 94;
majeczka 100; Zsolt, Biczó 101; Krisztina Farkas 102; Jane26 105; Johnny Lye 114c; lucadp 114b; Coprid 115; Mihai Simonia 116;
Valeriy Lebedev 117; Kushch Dmitry 119; Sebastian Duda 126; John Wollwerth 133; Chris Rawlins 162; Fotoline 186; Velychko 188;
phumphaosrk 194; salpics32 198; Goodluz 203; JohnKwan 207; rangizzz 210; Gemenacom 213; CandyBox Images 214; Max Baumann
220; Vladimir Koletic 223; Orange Line Media 231; hfng 234; Cheryl Casey 235; Sven Hoppe 237; Serhiy Kobyakov 238; Lisa S. 239;
JustASC 242; PHOTOCREO Michal Bednarek 243; woodygraphs 244; docent 245; elwynn 246; Constant 250.

HOW TO MAKE
MONEY
ON THE
INTERNET

ROB HAWKINS

Foreword by Howard Davies-Carr,
creator of 'Charlie Bit Me' YouTube hit

**FLAME TREE
PUBLISHING**

Contents

Find out all you need to know about selling your unwanted items via the internet. Whether you have an attic full of unwanted books and belongings, or want to sell the toys and bikes your children have out-grown, this chapter shows where on the internet such items can be sold, what's involved in selling them and how much it will cost. There are step-by-step guides to selling and lots of hints and tips to help.

Become a Pro Internet Seller

Selling items via the internet can become a full-time occupation. If you're keen to know what's involved in turning a part-time money-making venture into a large-scale business, this chapter reveals how eBay and Amazon can help and how much it will cost. If you already run a high-street shop or business and are considering selling on the internet, this chapter provides many of the answers you may be looking for.

The Logistics of Selling

There's more to selling on the internet than simply listing items for sale and waiting for the orders to come in. If you're serious about selling on the internet, there are a lot of logistical points that need to be considered and planned for. How do you deal with enquiries, deliveries abroad, returns and refunds? All these issues and more are covered in depth.

Make Money from Your Website....... 120

A popular approach to making money on the internet is to set up your own website and use it to generate income. This can be in the form of selling your own or other people's products, or selling advertising space. There are numerous solutions to generating income from your own website, but this chapter concentrates on the ones used by most people – selling and advertising.

Make a Website.................................... 150

If you have ideas for creating your own website and making money from it, but don't know how to create one, then this chapter covers all you need to know to get you started. Creating your own website has never been easier, with free software and online services that provide easy-to-follow step-by-step guides. This chapter outlines them all and enables you to quickly create your own website.

Other Money-making Ideas

Whilst the most popular methods of making money on the internet concern selling goods and selling advertising, there are many more solutions that can be equally profitable. This chapter outlines a number of them and gives real-life case studies where people have made money. Everything from completing online surveys to finding cashback and discount offers is covered in depth.

Legal Issues

The internet may have created numerous opportunities for businesses to seek customers from the far corners of the world, but there's also a downside to this free market. Fraud, scams and litigation are some of the real-life problems that surface every day, often costing businesses and individuals a lot of money. This chapter highlights many of the common legal problems and how best to avoid them. It also highlights the tax implications of earning money via the internet.

Foreword
Charlie Bit Me: Make Your Own Luck

The nature of modern communication has opened up a host of opportunities. In generations past, products and services were created, provided and consumed within a local area. People often didn't travel more than a few miles, even important and life changing information and news travelled slowly. Now even a simple family moment can be seen by hundreds of millions of people.

Charlie and Harry's video is a simple, innocent family moment which has caught the imagination and interest of people all over the planet. This was never our intention. However, due to our success it has opened up a source of income.

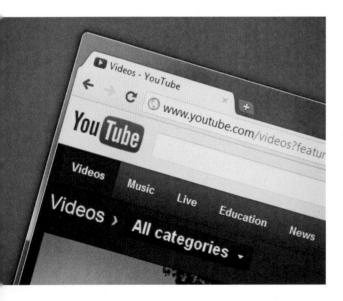

Thanks to the internet, any individual can now access anyone, anywhere in the world who could be a potential consumer of their product or service, regardless of location, currency or even language. This still relatively recent revolution in communications is especially exciting if you have something unique which can only achieve its money-making potential by reaching such a large and diverse audience. Of course it's not just about selling: if you have an interest or skill that draws people to your website, blog,

Facebook page, Twitter feeds etc., advertisers will pay to advertise alongside. There are many ways to generate income...

We have been lucky. Something we made and shared quite freely became a worldwide phenomenon. Our story has been retold in different languages all over the world. A colleague once said to me 'You make your own luck'. We did not set out to make money from YouTube, but without doubt decisions have been made along the way, which have contributed to our success. While you may only see a short family video, this belies hundreds of hours spent supporting its rise to fame. People from hundreds of countries have bought 'Charlie Bit Me' T-Shirts, and we will soon have a mobile app and will be producing new targeted content. However, we have been deliberately slow to exploit certain markets due to the nature of our material – we need to take into account the social and long-term impacts of what we do as a family.

We have embraced the nature of the market we have found ourselves in. Equally, we have been open to new ideas and possibilities that became available. We talk to people all over the world, via the internet, such as on social sites and by email – as well as on the television, the phone and by video conference.

The point is that, even as an individual, you have the power to achieve your goals by embracing opportunities that come along and making the most of what you have. Is our story repeatable? Who knows, but all the tools are available to help you realize your dreams and 'make your own luck'.

Howard Davies-Carr
Creator of 'Charlie Bit Me' YouTube hit

Introduction

The internet is a worldwide market that originated in the latter half of the twentieth century. For many people and businesses, it became a serious method of making money during the beginning of the twenty-first century. It has evolved with numerous ways of making money, some that can potentially make you rich and others that will create a small amount of extra income. This book explores the popular methods of making money from the internet, showing you what's involved.

Endless Opportunities

There are seemingly an infinite number of ideas for making money via the internet, and you don't have to trawl very many web pages before you're presented with money-making schemes, success stories and courses and books that promise to tell you how to become a millionaire from a few simple clicks of your mouse. However, it's not always as easy as it sounds, and many ideas are saturated with many people trying their hand. Making money from the internet requires a realistic approach. Using the advice and resources outlined in this book, you can start off creating some extra income and work on bigger plans as you learn new skills and find better opportunities.

Popular Money Makers

The ways to make money from the internet generally centre around two traditional activities – selling and advertising. These are the staple money-making resources of most media businesses, including newspapers and television programmes. In the case of the internet, the subjects of selling and advertising have numerous off-shoots, but these are the main core business activities that can generate income. Selling can involve goods that are sold through a variety of websites (eBay, Amazon, classifieds, or your own website), but the goods can range from real-life objects to virtual items, such as an e-book or app for a mobile device. The same can apply to advertising, where commission can be generated on sales or money earned via click-throughs.

Virtual Money Makers

The internet has generated a wide range of money-making ideas that don't exist in the real world. For instance, you can buy an image and display it on your mobile phone, or you can buy an e-book and read it on a Kindle, smartphone or computer. Many of these virtual products and methods of making money are explored in this book with clear information on how you can earn money yourself.

Attracting Attention

If you want to make a lot of money from the internet, there is one aspect above all that needs to be successful – marketing.

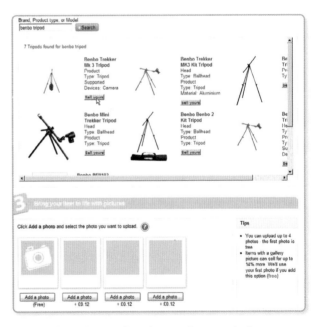

Above: Selling websites such as eBay provide easy methods of listing items for sale. Step-by-step guides to listing items are covered in chapter one of this book.

Whether you're running a website, selling stuff via eBay or writing a blog, the key to success is to make sure you draw lots of attention. The various methods of promotion via the internet are clearly outlined in this book, as it is one of the key elements of success.

Direct and Indirect Attention

There are numerous indirect activities on the internet which help to contribute towards making money, and many of these are covered in this book. Blogs, posting comments on forums, broadcasting videos, Tweeting and having a presence on Facebook can all raise your profile or the profile of your business and help to point potential customers in the right direction. In many cases, it is these activities that provide the key to success and often require time and commitment.

Above: Businesses can use eBay to sell multiple items and set up a virtual shop. Chapter two covers what's involved in professional selling.

Seven Chapters

The many topics relating to making money from the internet are outlined over seven chapters in this book. The most popular money-making activity, selling your stuff, is covered in chapter one, with details relating to eBay and other selling sites. If you're interested in becoming a professional seller, then chapter two outlines what's involved, and chapter three looks at the practicalities and logistics of full-time selling. Whilst selling is one of the most popular methods of making money from the internet, another angle is to establish a website and use a number of ideas to generate income from it. This is covered in depth in chapter four, and from a practical angle of creating a

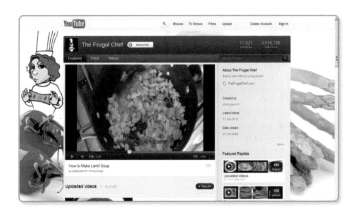

Left: YouTube has attracted millions of viewers and diverted them to specific websites, such as this one for The Frugal Chef.

website in chapter five. The penultimate chapter deals with a round-up of many other money-making ideas, ranging from online surveys to broadcasting videos with advertising. Finally, chapter seven covers the subjects you may want to avoid, but need to know, including the potential for fraud, how to protect customer information, whether you should pay tax and how to identify scams.

Small Chunks

Flick through the pages of this book and you will see short paragraphs throughout, each describing particular subjects with sub-headings where necessary. Within each of the seven chapters in this book, main topics are covered over at least two pages and, in

Above: Creating your own website couldn't be simpler and chapter five shows exactly how it can be done online for free.

most cases, no more than six pages. Any subject that is especially complicated is covered either as easy-to-read points or as a simple step-by-step guide. You won't have to spend hours reading several pages to gain an understanding in a subject such as becoming a top-rated seller on eBay.

Above: One of the easiest ways to make a little cash from the internet is to complete online surveys.

Flick and Pick

There is no need to read this book all the way through from start to finish. Just pick a topic you wish to read, find it within its respective chapter (see the index at the back of this book for a list of topics) and you can read just that section.

Step-by-step

Throughout this book there are several step-by-step guides showing how to create a website online, create a blog and sell items on eBay. These step-by-step guides are designed to be easy to follow and contain straightforward information that can be revisited again and again. Each step-by-step guide is accompanied by illustrations.

Hot Tips and Did You Know?

Look out for the Hot Tips and Did You Know? boxes scattered throughout the pages of this book. These offer advice and useful snippets of information on various matters relating to making money from the internet.

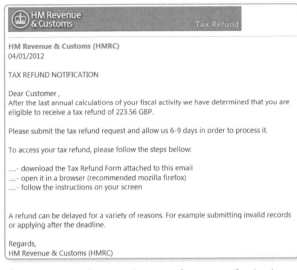

HM Revenue & Customs — Tax Refund

HM Revenue & Customs (HMRC)
04/01/2012

TAX REFUND NOTIFICATION

Dear Customer ,
After the last annual calculations of your fiscal activity we have determined that you are eligible to receive a tax refund of 223.56 GBP.

Please submit the tax refund request and allow us 6-9 days in order to process it.

To access your tax refund, please follow the steps bellow:

.....- download the Tax Refund Form attached to this email
.....- open it in a browser (recommended mozilla firefox)
.....- follow the instructions on your screen

A refund can be delayed for a variety of reasons. For example submitting invalid records or applying after the deadline.

Regards,
HM Revenue & Customs (HMRC)

Above: The internet has opened up a can of worms over fraud and scams, which are outlined in chapter seven.

Help!

If you're stuck on a particular topic contained in this book, please email Flame Tree Publishing at support@ flametreepublishing.com. We cannot operate a 24-hour helpline for all your internet needs, but we will answer your query via email and try to provide as much useful information as possible.

Get Rich Quickly or Slowly

There are plenty of books, courses and websites promising the secrets that will enable you to unlock the key to becoming a millionaire from seemingly very little effort. This book is not one of them, but it does offer practical advice about numerous money-making methods that could generate a significant amount of income from the internet. Whether you want to have a go at selling some items on eBay, or start to develop a comprehensive website with affiliate advertising, social networking links and sophisticated marketing tools, this book provides many of the resources and practical information to guide you through what's involved.

Sell Your Stuff

Planning to Sell

One of the simplest ways of making money on the internet is to advertise and sell unwanted items. But how much should you sell them for, when should you sell, how will the items be delivered or collected and who will buy them? The following pages provide the answers.

What Have You Got to Sell?

Before the internet, unwanted items were usually sold by placing an advertisement in the classified-ads section of the local paper, or by sticking a postcard-sized notice in the window of the post office or newsagent, or on the noticeboard of the local community centre. The internet has opened up a whole new market (a global one in some cases) and created a potentially vast audience of buyers. However, the first concern before you start thinking about selling, is listing the goods that you want to sell. If you've raided the shed or attic and found a wide assortment of unwanted items, note down their exact details and don't sell them yet. First, it's important to determine their potential value and work out the best way of selling them, giving thought to whether they can be delivered or collected.

Hot Tip

Honesty pays. If you are trying to sell something that is defective, such as a bike with a broken chain, make sure potential buyers are aware of this.

Research

The starting point for selling items is to arm yourself with plenty of information and knowledge about the best ways and best times to sell. Speak to any experienced market trader or shop owner and they will know what type of stock sells well at particular times of the year, who their customers are, and what prices these customers are willing to pay.

Pricing

Deciding on the price you want to sell an item for isn't always easy. You may have paid a reasonable price for a bicycle five years ago, but it may only be worth a tenth of its value now. The easiest way to fix on a price is to look for similar items that have sold and find out how much they sold for. Websites such

Above: Searching for completed listings in eBay can help to determine how much a particular item has sold for in the past.

as eBay allow you to search for items that have been sold by selecting 'Completed listings' down the left side of the screen. It's also helpful to look for similar items that are currently for sale to help determine whether you should sell on the same website at a cheaper price.

New to Old

Sometimes, second-hand prices of equivalents may not be available, so it might prove difficult to ascertain a reasonable selling price. If this is the case, find out if the item is still available to purchase brand new and how much it sells for. In many situations, sellers calculate the second-hand price as around 50% of the brand new price, but check for versions, editions and updates, which may affect the value of your item. For instance, a first edition of a book is usually worth more than a later edition.

Valuable and Collectible

Where an item is of collectible interest or appreciating value, it's important to arm yourself with as much information about it to ensure potential buyers are assured they are buying a genuine product. If possible, look at the same items for sale elsewhere and find the features that are highlighted in the description. Does it help to have the original packaging or specific accessories? Are there any serial numbers or manufacturer's markings that signify a genuine item? Can you obtain any information from a collector or auction house to confirm a product is genuine and collectible?

Above: The bidding history of an auctioned item on eBay can be viewed throughout the auction; use this to observe the behaviour of potential buyers.

Auction Behaviour

If you can find items already selling that are similar to what you have to sell, it's worth spending a few days watching the auctions. Look at the history of the bidding to see whether all the bids are placed at the very end of the auction.
See how many different bids are made and, although you won't be able to see who bids, you can see the number of people bidding.

Hot Tip

An item can be watched on eBay by selecting it from the results listing, then click on the button labelled 'Add to Watch list'.

Timing

Selling an artificial Christmas tree during summer isn't going to be as easy as selling it during the weeks

leading up to 25 December. Whilst some goods are in greater demand according to the season and weather, it may be less easy to determine the best time to sell others. Expensive items that are not obvious gifts may be easier to sell if you avoid times of the year when most people have large expenditure to outlay, such as around and after Christmas and during July and August, when many people are on holiday.

Timing and Competition

If the marketplace in which you want to sell your product or products is already flooded with similar goods, this might not represent a good opportunity. That said, you may be able to turn this to your advantage, if, for instance, you sell at a cheaper price than the competition and offer more features or accessories to gain a competitive advantage. For instance, if you are selling an electronic toy, but don't want to offer a cheaper price than the rest of the similar toys for sale, include extras such as batteries and accessories.

Delivery or Collection

It's essential to decide whether you want to deliver an item you are selling or insist that the buyer collects. In the case of delivery, you may want to use a courier service or a similar service with a traceable delivery. This will help ensure the item is delivered, minimizing the risk of the buyer claiming they have not received their goods (which can affect your ratings on eBay and other selling sites). However, it's important to calculate the cost of delivery and state this when selling the item, so you don't lose out on postage costs.

Collection Capers

If an item you are selling is simply too large, difficult, heavy or fragile to post, then it's important to stress that collection in person is the only method. However, be prepared for buyers to insist that a bicycle, for example, can be dismantled and boxed for collection by a courier. Even if the buyer arranges the collection, you will still have to source the packaging and box the item.

Above: This slide and climbing frame are going to be far too big to parcel up and post, so it's essential to state that the buyer must collect.

> ## Hot Tip
>
> Don't try to make a profit on postage. Some buyers are dissuaded by high delivery costs.

Setting up to Sell on eBay

eBay is one of the internet's most successful websites for selling unwanted, second-hand and new items, ranging from toys and computer equipment to bicycles and cars. If you want to sell your own items on eBay, there are a few things you must do before you begin selling, including registering and choosing a payment method. The following pages guide you through what's involved.

Register with eBay

You have to create an account with eBay before you can start selling items through it. Depending on where you live in the world, eBay has a website relative to your country. For example, if you live in the UK, then visit www.ebay.co.uk, whereas if you live in the USA, visit www.ebay.com, and if you live in Australia, visit www.ebay.com.au. Some of these websites are slightly different, but in all cases there will be a 'register' button near the centre of the screen. Click on this to create an account with eBay.

Above: Personal details have to be entered when registering with eBay, but they are not disclosed or shared without your consent.

Enter Your Personal Details

It's important to enter your details accurately and avoid any false information. You will need an email address that doesn't have an eBay account connected to it. Choose a suitable user ID for yourself, which is at least six characters long, but be prepared to try a few variations as someone may have already taken the name you want to use. Don't forget to read through any user agreements and privacy policies to make sure you are happy to register

Did You Know?

Your User ID for your eBay account is displayed when you sell items, so choose one that is relevant and certainly not offensive.

with eBay. According to the registration web page, eBay does not rent or sell your personal information to third parties without your consent.

User ID Don'ts

An eBay user ID cannot include spaces or tabs, special characters or symbols (for example, £ or &), but can include asterisks, underscores, full stops and dashes. Your first or last name cannot be used along with email or website addresses.

Password Pointers

You will need to think of a suitable password to go with your eBay account. This will enable you to log in to your eBay account and sell items. eBay has some rules and helpful advice concerning passwords, which are as follows:

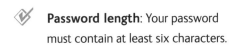

Password length: Your password must contain at least six characters.

Symbols and letters: The password should contain at least two of the following – upper-case or lower-case letters, numbers or special characters such as a question/exclamation mark, underscore or @ symbol.

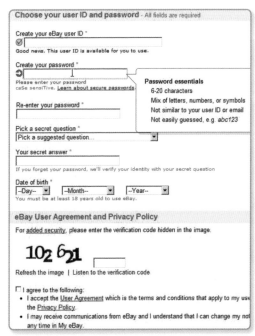

Above: eBay has a number of rules concerning passwords to help prevent fraud.

ID or email: Do not use your email address or eBay user ID as the password.

 Obvious words: Avoid using obvious passwords, such as 'abc123' or 'Password'.

 Personal stuff: Don't use personal information that can easily be guessed, such as your name, phone number, or date of birth.

Identity Confirmation

After entering your personal details and clicking on the 'Continue' button, the next screen to appear may inform you that eBay needs to confirm your identity. This can be completed by either asking eBay to telephone you, or by entering details of your bank, credit or debit card. If you choose to request eBay to telephone you, an automatic phone call will be made to you (landline only)

> ## Hot Tip
> Replace letters for numbers in a password. For instance, a password such as 'London' could replace the 'o' for a zero to become 'L0nd0n'.

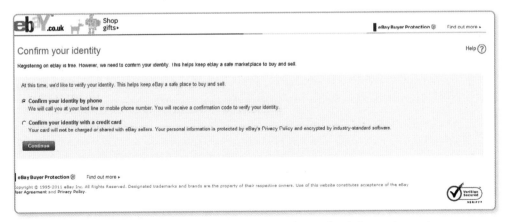

Above: Registering with eBay requires you to confirm your identity either via the telephone or by entering your bank, credit or debit card details.

and a four-digit verification code will be read out. You will need to enter this code on eBay's website to complete registration. If you choose to enter your credit or debit card details, complete the relevant fields. eBay states that it does not use these details for any other purpose than confirming your identity.

Paying for eBay Fees

eBay requires a method of payment to be set up to enable you to pay for advertising items and to pay any commission and other fees when an item has been sold. There are a number of different methods of payment, which are explained as follows:

- **PayPal**: This has become a popular method of payment with a reputation for reliable and secure transactions. You have to create a PayPal account and either enter your bank, credit or debit card details. This will be used to extract payments or credit funds when you sell something through eBay. For further details, visit www.paypal.com.

- **Direct Debit**: Bank or Building Society account details need to be supplied to eBay and eBay will automatically send a request to your financial institution to deduct any fees for selling items. This type of payment takes roughly 19 days to set up.

- **Credit card**: Enter your Visa or MasterCard credit card details online via eBay and payments will be taken each month for any fees incurred when selling items.

- **Cheque or postal order**: eBay can issue an invoice and payment can be made via a cheque or postal order. Once eBay receives the cheque or postal order, allow seven to 10 business days for the payment to clear.

Receiving Payments

Items you sell through eBay need to be paid for and there are a number of methods of receiving payments. These include the following:

- **PayPal**: All eBay sellers must offer PayPal as a payment method. This is a secure online payment method, which allows you to get paid quickly without sharing any of your financial information with the buyer. As a seller, the disadvantage of being paid using PayPal is that it incurs a fee (*see* Calculate Your Fees, page 29).

- **Cheque or postal order**: This is one of the lengthiest methods of payment as it is best to wait until the cheque or postal order has cleared before posting or releasing the sold item. However, this method avoids fees incurred with PayPal.

- **Credit or debit card**: If you operate a business that can take credit or debit card payments, then this method can be used to receive payment for an item sold through eBay. However, this type of sale incurs a fee, just like PayPal.

- **Pay on collection**: Most sellers prefer this method of payment, especially where the buyer collects or the seller delivers in person. No fees are incurred via eBay for this type of payment.

eBay Fees

Once you have an account with eBay, selling items through the website is very straightforward. However, some careful planning is required to help ensure you get the right price and keep any fees as low as possible. The following pages outline the different approaches to selling through eBay and how much it will cost.

Auction, Buy Now, Make Offer

There are a number of ways of selling an item through eBay, all of which can help to sell it for a reasonable price. These include the following:

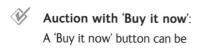 **Auction**: This is one of the most popular methods of selling an item. It allows interested buyers to bid for a limited period of time. The highest bidder wins the auction when it ends and buys the item.

Auction with reserve: A reserve price can be set. This incurs an additional fee (*see* Calculate Your Fees, page 29), but prevents your item from being sold too cheaply. In some countries, there is a minimum reserve price, whereas others have no such rules.

Item condition:	**Used**
Time left:	**2m 51s** (25 Nov. 2011 08:51:46 GMT)
Current bid:	**£140.00** [1 bid]
	Reserve not met
	Enter £142.00 or more Place bid
Price:	**£196.00** Buy it now

Above: This eBay auction includes a reserve price and a 'Buy it now' option. The seller has to pay for these, but it often helps to ensure the item doesn't sell too cheaply and an interested buyer can purchase instead of bidding.

Auction with 'Buy it now': A 'Buy it now' button can be

displayed alongside your item, which often tempts people who really want to secure the item and would rather not take the gamble of losing out in an auction.

Classified ad: Items can be sold on eBay with a fixed price. This is popular for high-value items such as a car or property. A fixed fee is payable, depending on what is being sold.

Make offer: This is often available with items that are listed for sale in a classified ad. It allows interested buyers to suggest a price to pay and wait for the seller to accept or decline the offer.

Hot Tip

Carefully calculate the total fees for a number of different ways of selling an item on eBay before deciding which one is best.

Calculate Your Fees

It's important to be aware of the costs incurred when selling an item through eBay. In some cases these can easily escalate and the final costs can be more than the profit you had hoped to gain from the sale. The fees depend on what you are selling and how you want to sell it. Here are the fees that may be incurred:

Insertion fee: General items (not cars, holidays or property) incur an insertion fee ranging from free to around £1.30 or $2 (or whatever the equivalent currency of your country), depending on the starting price. Large items such as a car or property have a higher fee (in the UK, a car currently costs £10–14.99 and property costs £35).

Buy it now: Can be included in an item for auction and usually costs 20–40 pence or, in some cases, is free. Exceptions include large items such as a car where a 'Buy it now' price costs roughly the same as an insertion fee.

Reserve price: eBay charges 1–3% of the reserve price, although in some countries this is free up to a specific amount. If a reserve price is included, the insertion fee is based upon this value, not the starting price. In some countries, a maximum fee for the reserve price is applied.

Sale price (final value): eBay charges 9–10% of the final value up to a specific maximum, depending on the country. High value items such as cars are charged at a particular amount.

PayPal: If your buyer pays via PayPal, then PayPal will charge a fee for handling the transaction. It charges roughly 20p or $0.30 per transaction, then between 1.4% and 3.4% of the sale price (final value), depending on the amount. In some countries, a fixed percentage is charged for each transaction.

> ## Did You Know?
> eBay occasionally holds promotional offers where insertion fees are free or other fees are reduced.

The Cost of Selling on eBay in the UK

Selling a collectible book through eBay with a starting price of £15 will incur an insertion fee of 50p. If the auction ends at £35, then eBay will charge 10%, which comes to £3.50. If the buyer pays via PayPal, then PayPal will charge 20p plus 3.4% of £35, which is £1.19. So although the book sold for £35, you will be paid £29.61 because the fees amount to £5.39. There are also further additional (optional) fees if you include more than one photograph when selling an item and use other selling tools. These are covered later in this chapter.

Watch Those Fees

Sometimes it's easy to get carried away with all the bells and whistles of selling on eBay, which can help to tempt buyers into purchasing. However, it can become expensive, especially for low-value goods. Add together the cost of an insertion fee, reserve price, extra photographs, a colourful theme, the commission fee for postage and the 9–10% charged on the final price, and you can easily see the total fees exceeding 20% of the value of the sale.

eBay Planning

When you're ready to sell something on eBay, don't make a start until you've planned and researched everything from a suitable category and description to photographs, pricing and contact details. Sales on eBay frequently fail because an item is wrongly categorized or photographs are missing. Poor planning leads to poor performance.

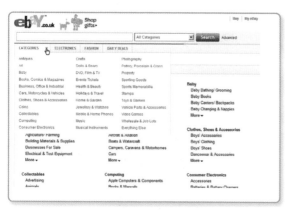

Above: eBay divides items for sale into different categories, which makes them easier to find. Make sure that anything you sell is under the most appropriate category.

Which Category?

One of the key points to ensuring potential buyers find your item for sale on eBay is to make sure it's under the most appropriate category. Buyers will often only search within a specific category to help narrow the results, so you need to find the category where similar items are for sale and make sure you select this one when placing your item for sale. This is covered in more detail with a step-by-step guide to selling something on eBay in the next section of this chapter.

Descriptive Title

Decide upon a suitable title for the item you are selling. This will appear in the results listing if a potential buyer is looking for something that fits your title description. In some cases, eBay can provide such a title, but it's worthwhile researching the titles used by other people selling similar items. The title should include the manufacturer's name and any relevant information such as model name or specification. However, the title can only contain a maximum of 80 characters.

Description

This is one area of eBay selling that requires a lot of careful thought and planning. Look at descriptions of other items on eBay, especially of products that you would like to buy, to see which descriptions inspire confidence in buying and which ones put you off. Many descriptions are cluttered with coloured and different-sized text that can look amateurish. Some descriptions contain standard text from eBay or the manufacturer. Think about what you would like to read if you were buying your item from someone you had never met before and consider the following:

- **Condition**: Be honest about the condition of the item and whether there is any damage.

- **Length of ownership**: If you have owned the item for a long time or since it was new, include this information in the description.

- **Use**: If you are selling something that has hardly been used and has been well kept, for example, stored in the loft, try to include this in the description. Similarly, if the item has been used everyday but has never let you down, this is also worth mentioning.

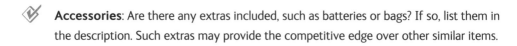

Accessories: Are there any extras included, such as batteries or bags? If so, list them in the description. Such extras may provide the competitive edge over other similar items.

Original packaging: If the box or packaging that accompanied the item when it was new is included in the sale, make sure you state this in the description. Buyers often perceive you have taken good care of the item if you still have its original packaging.

User manual: Any instructions, manuals or other literature relating to the item that is useful for potential buyers should be clearly outlined in the description.

Photographs

One photograph can be included for free with an item (it's part of the insertion fee), but in some cases, it may be worthwhile including more images. Up to 12 photographs or images can be added, which each cost a fixed amount to add (12p each in the UK and $0.15 in the USA), but look out for offers to include a block or pack of photos. There are also offers for making photos stand out with enlargement and zoom features. Look at other similar items for sale on eBay and see how many images are included, plus whether or not it will help to have more images. If you're selling a poster, for example, one image is probably sufficient, but if you are selling a dinner set, you may want to take photographs of sets of plates and any damaged items.

> ### Hot Tip
> Divide description information into lists and bullet points to make it easier to read.

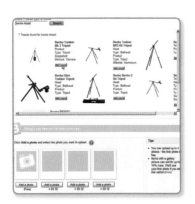

Above: eBay has a number of stock photographs for a range of products, which can be included in an auction.

eBay Images

eBay has some stock images of particular products, which can be included with the sale of your item. These images are automatically displayed when creating a listing; once you have selected a title description, the images will appear (see the next section for detailed instructions on creating a listing).

Take Your Own Photos

You can include your own photos when selling something on eBay. This requires careful planning to ensure the photograph is clear, in focus and the right size. The following list provides some hints and tips for creating images to accompany a listing on eBay:

- **Clear background**: Don't photograph the item for sale with lots of junk in the background. If it can be moved, position it against a clear backdrop.

- **Contrasting background**: Don't photograph a white object you want to sell against a white background, as it will be difficult to see. Instead, use a contrasting, dark-coloured background.

- **Lighting**: Try to photograph the item in daylight. If your camera has a flash, this will help to brighten up the item for sale, but it may also produce glare and bright spots on items such as a TV or set of wine glasses.

Clear composition: Don't try to be too artistic with your photographs. Straightforward shots of the front, back and sides of an item for sale are what most potential buyers are looking for.

Show the damage: If an item for sale is damaged, try to photograph this. Potential buyers like honesty.

Steady the camera: If you have a tripod, use it to reduce camera shake that may result in a blurred image. If you don't have a tripod, secure the camera on a flat surface and if it has a timer, use this to reduce camera shake.

Picture quality: If possible, set the image quality to medium or low to produce an image of roughly 1024x768 pixels (less than 1 megapixel). This is sufficient for eBay.

Editing Photographs

eBay provides some simple editing tools to help crop, rotate and adjust the brightness of photographs. However, you may want to use image-editing software or the software provided with your digital camera to further enhance the image, add text or make sure it is the correct file size. The following pointers provide some useful advice:

> **Hot Tip**
>
> Flat objects, such as stamps or CD covers can be scanned to create an image of them.

Crop to size: Whilst cropping an image will help to remove unwanted items and make sure the item is clearly displayed, avoid cropping to awkward dimensions. eBay provides a square box on the left side of the screen to display images, so try to crop an image to make the width and height the same.

File size: eBay recommends the image should be at least 1000 pixels along the longest side of the image (width or height or both).

Adjust brightness and contrast: Make sure the brightness of the image is sufficient to be able to clearly see the item for sale. Try adjusting both the brightness and contrast. In most cases, increase the brightness and reduce the contrast or vice versa.

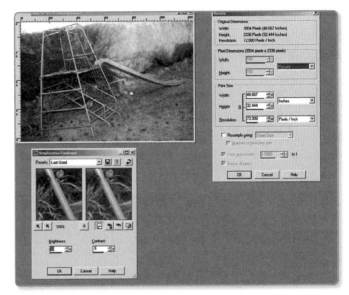

Above: The size, brightness and contrast of a photo can be adjusted in most image-editing programs to ensure it's suitable for using on eBay.

Add text: If you want to highlight some damage on an item for sale, try adding text to the image.

Original images: Keep a copy of the original images of the item for sale, just in case you make a mess of editing them.

Filenames: Use filenames that are easy to remember and relevant. This may help to retrieve images in the future and reuse them if you sell the same item again.

Hot Tip

Photos saved as JPG images are suitable for including in an eBay listing.

Step-by-step Selling on eBay

Placing your first listing on eBay can be a nail-biting experience as you hope you've got all the facts correct, but it's all very straightforward and mistakes can be easily corrected. The following step-by-step guide provides clear and concise information about what's involved.

 Click on 'Sell': Go to www.ebay.com (or the relevant eBay website for your country), log in and click on 'Sell' near the top of the screen. From the menu that drops down, select 'Sell an item'. The screen will change and a simple description box will be displayed.

 Describe your item: Enter a word or a few words that best represent the name or title of the item you want to sell. eBay will automatically search for suitable titles and may list a few suggestions.

Enter an EAN or keywords that describe your item.

| dining room table and chairs | Start selling |

For example: Amethyst gemstone rings

◉ Quick sell (not suitable for vehicles)
List your item quickly using the most popular options

○ Advanced sell (Sell your item form)
Access to all the options (subtitle, listing designer and r

Browse categories | Recently used categories

🚗 Sell a car or motorbike

Above: Once you've logged in, selling something on eBay takes a matter of minutes.

 Start selling: Once you've typed in a title description of the item you want to sell, click on the button labelled 'Start selling'. The screen will change and a number of boxes and steps will appear.

 Find a category: eBay will in most cases automatically list some categories that apply to the item you are selling. Under section 2 of the selling page, any suggested categories and sub-categories will be listed and they can be selected from here. However, if

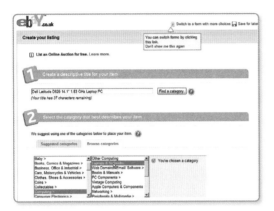

Above: eBay can automatically identify certain products you are selling and ensure it is placed in the correct category.

Above: Some products can be displayed with standard technical information on eBay.

there are no suitable categories, click on the 'Browse categories' tab and choose one from the list.

 Include product information: If eBay has helped to automatically select a particular item according to its make and model, it may provide some product information about it. You can choose whether to include this information at no extra cost.

 Add photos: One photograph can be included for free with a listing and up to 11 additional photos can be included with an additional cost for each one. If eBay has helped to automatically select a particular item according to its make and model, then it may also provide a choice of stock images for you to use. Otherwise, click on the 'Add a photo' button and another window will appear. Click on 'Choose file' to locate an image on your computer, then upload it.

Did You Know?

You can partially create a listing and save it, then return to it later. Just click on 'Save for later', near the top of the screen.

Above: In many cases when creating a listing, eBay provides a variety of drop-down boxes to help determine the condition of the item you are selling.

Describe your item: Complete any drop-down lists and tick boxes to help describe the specification and condition of the item you are selling. This is all contained in section 4 of the selling page. At the bottom of this section, there is a large box in which to type your own text. Choose suitable fonts, sizes and colours.

Set a price and postage: We covered pricing earlier in this chapter. Under section 5 of the selling page, you can set a starting price, a duration for the auction (one to 10 days), an optional 'Buy it now' price, when you want the auction to start, and how much postage will cost (if applicable).

Payment: PayPal has to be included as a method of payment for your listing, but you can also include others such as cash on collection or cheque/postal order. These choices are available under section 6 of the selling page.

Save and preview: Once you have completed all sections of the selling page, click on the 'Save and preview' button near the bottom of the screen. You can then inspect the listing, make changes and, finally, complete it.

More Selling Choices

If you want to customize your listing and find more options, there is a different screen in eBay that can be used to list an item for sale. When you begin to place a listing, there's an option for 'Advanced sell'. Alternatively, if you are halfway through using the selling page mentioned in the previous section, click on the option near the top of the screen, labelled 'Switch to a form with more choices'.

Bulleted and Numbered Lists

Under the 'Advanced sell' or after switching to a form with more choices, the description box can include bulleted and numbered lists with indented and out-dented sections. This can help to create easy-to-read information about the item you are selling.

Above: The advanced selling page in eBay allows you to include bulleted and numbered lists, colourful themes and visitor counters at no extra cost.

Add a Theme

eBay listings lack background colour, but this can be added for a few pence or cents extra (around 7p in the UK) with a theme. This is below the description area in the advanced listing screen. Make sure the relevant check box is ticked, then choose a theme and design. You can also add a visitor counter, which helps to show potential buyers how many people have looked at the item.

Setting a Reserve Price

A reserve price can only be set in the advanced selling screen and is near the lower half of the page, amongst the choices for starting price and duration. By default, no reserve price is set, but you can set a reserve price by clicking on the 'Change' option. A separate window will appear allowing you to enter a reserve price and see information concerning listing fees (usually, eBay will charge 1–3% of the reserve price on top of all its other fees). Click on 'Save' to confirm the reserve price and return to the previous screen.

Online Classifieds

There are a number of worldwide, nationwide and local websites that can help to sell items, ranging from online classified advertising to posting advertisements on a forum. Many of these website are free to advertise items for sale and have categories and location searches to ensure potential buyers will find you, whilst others charge fees or commission, but take the hassle out of selling.

Gumtree

Established in 2000 in the UK, Gumtree (www.gumtree.com) was initially set up to bring together a variety of free classified advertisements in London, ranging from unwanted goods to cars, services and property to buy or rent. Gumtree now covers 48 cities in the UK and Ireland, offering easy-to-follow search methods

Left: Gumtree is a useful online classified-ads website that can help find potential buyers locally and nationally.

for finding items and similarly easy-to-follow procedures on placing advertisements. Whilst standard advertisements for selling an item are free and last for 60 days, there are optional features to help promote an advertisement, which cost between £4.95 and £19.95.

General Classifieds

There are dozens of websites offering free classified advertisements. It's not particularly easy trying to choose which ones will prove worthwhile. Searching through these websites for the item you are selling may help to determine whether it's a popular seller (especially if you can look at old sales), but it may be worth listing your item on as many of these sites as possible to find your buyer. The following list outlines some of the free-to-advertise classified websites in the UK:

- www.itsmymarket.com
- www.friday-ad.co.uk
- www.freeads.co.uk
- www.classifieds.co.uk

- www.adtrader.co.uk
- www.preloved.co.uk
- www.vivastreet.co.uk

Classifieds in the USA

- www.usfreeads.com
- www.inetgiant.com
- www.classifiedsforfree.com

- www.usnetads.com
- www.olclassifieds.com
- www.telists.com

Local Newspapers

If you want to sell an item locally (perhaps you don't want to or can't post it), your local newspaper may have online classified advertisements, which are also included in the paper edition of their newspaper. In some cases, there will be a charge for placing an advertisement.

Specialized Classifieds

Some items are best sold through specialist websites that only provide classified advertisements for that type of good. Autotrader, for example, has gained a reputation for being one of the most successful online classified websites for selling cars and has websites relevant to a number of countries (www.autotrader.co.uk for the UK and www.autotrader.com for the USA).

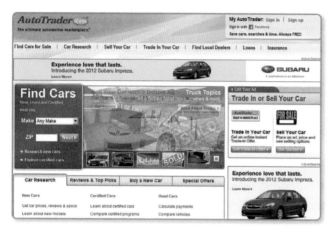

Above: Autotrader has become a useful website in the UK, USA and other countries for selling cars, trucks, vans and motorcycles.

Selling Through Forums and Clubs

If there is an owners' club, register or similar organization for a specific hobby or interest relating to what you are trying to sell, then there will generally be a relevant website with classified advertisements or a forum that offers classified advertisements. These are usually free to join (registration is often necessary to avoid unsuitable advertisements) and can often help to value what you are selling and find a buyer.

Social Network Selling

The emergence of social networking websites including Facebook, Twitter, LinkedIn, Bebo and Friendster has seen the internet evolve into a whole new way of doing business. Whilst these websites were initially established to help people keep in contact, with revenue gained from advertising, a development has been to allow members to sell their stuff, even if it's just amongst their friends. Facebook has already started with its own members' classified listings using a feature called Garage Sale.

Garage Sale on Facebook

Garage Sale allows Facebook members to post personal items for sale directly on their profile page and buy items from friends. By adding this feature to the profile page, listings of items for sale can be created, allowing friends to look through them. Providing a buyer has entered their credit card details into their Facebook account, they can purchase items and leave Facebook to sort out the payment. The seller receives the funds via PayPal or a cheque. Garage Sale is operated by the internet retailer Buy.com, which charges 5% commission on the total selling price, so if you don't sell, you don't get charged.

Online Buyers

Some goods can be sold to specialists or people whose business is to buy and sell goods. Products range from MP3 players and digital cameras to mobile phones and games consoles. Whilst this may not be as profitable as selling something yourself, it can take the hassle out of selling. The following pages outline some of the specialists and markets available to quickly sell your unwanted items.

Sell an Old Mobile Phone

There are a number of organizations willing to purchase old mobile phones, and websites such as www.mobilevaluer.com and www.o2recycle.co.uk help to determine which one will offer you the best price. In most cases, a price is agreed online and if you accept, a pre-paid jiffy bag is posted to you in which you send in the phone and await further contact and payment. CeX, for

Above: Martin Lewis' mobile phone valuation website at mobilevaluer.com can help you find the best deal when selling an old mobile phone to an online organization.

Hot Tip
When assessing the condition of an item you want to sell, be honest about any defects to avoid disappointment.

example, which operates in the USA, UK, Ireland and other countries, sells a variety of electronic goods (including mobile phones) and displays selling, trade in and exchange prices for different products. Visit www.webuy.com and you will be directed to the relevant website for your country

Trade in CDs and DVDs

There are lots of websites that offer to buy unwanted music and films on CD and DVD. In most cases, the album or film can be identified according to its barcode (this can sometimes be scanned via an iPhone) and a price is instantly displayed. If you agree to sell, either a free or pre-paid postage label can be printed and you then have to post the CD or DVD. Once the item has been inspected to make sure it works, payment is made via cheque or other means such as PayPal. Popular websites include www.webuy.com, www.musicmagpie.co.uk, www.tradeyourstuff.co.uk, www.secondspin.com and www.selldvdsonline.com.

Sell Games and Consoles

Some online specialists buy games and consoles, ranging from the compact Nintendo DS and Sony PlayStation Portable (PSP) to the larger Wii, Xbox and PS3. Specialists appear to operate in different countries and are not worldwide. For instance, in the UK, there is www.gadgetpanda.co.uk, www.swapgame.com (games only) and www.o2recycle.co.uk; in the USA there is www.buymytronics.com, www.gamestop.com (also in the UK) and www.gazelle.com. Many of these online buyers will also buy other electronic goods.

Instant eBay Sales in the USA

eBay in the USA (www.ebay.com) offers a buying service through AllTechWholesale to buy electronic devices such as cameras, MP3 players, smartphones, laptops, iPods, GPS equipment and similar items. Once a form is completed online (where an instant sale offer is calculated), a free shipping label has to be printed and the item posted. It is assessed upon receipt and payment made via PayPal (you must have a PayPal and eBay account) within five working days. This service is only currently available to residents within the USA. It can be found on www.eBay.com by clicking on 'Sell' near the top of the screen and selecting 'Instant sale' from the menu that drops down.

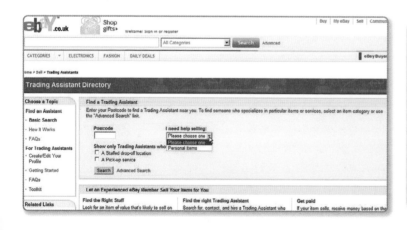

Hot Tip.

You can find a list of eBay Trading Assistants near you by entering your postcode or zip code in the Trading Assistant Directory.

eBay Trading Assistants

If you don't want to set up an account on eBay and sell items yourself, you can use a third party to sell them for you. This is known on eBay as a Trading Assistant (covered in depth in chapter two, Become a Pro Internet Seller) and is a type of eBay business that sells items for other people. The Trading Assistant charges a percentage commission to sell items and is bound by specific rules set by eBay.

Success Story – Stuff U Sell

Stuff U Sell (www.stuffusell.co.uk) is the largest Trading Assistant in the UK and was founded in 2004. They sell a wide range of items from DVDs to fitted kitchens, both second-hand goods for individuals and end-of-line stock for businesses. With collections arranged across the UK via courier or Stuff U Sell's own van in the South East, items are brought to the company's Park Royal warehouse and prepared for selling on eBay. The sales process starts with detailed research and assessment of items (offering a free service to recycle or donate to charity any unsaleable items) and continues

through a series of eBay listings, all managed by Stuff U Sell. Sellers are kept updated throughout the sales process and paid by BACS or cheque at the end. The charge (commission) for the service is based on the final value minus any eBay and PayPal fees, with a fee of one third up to £500 (minimum commission £10), dropping to 10% on net sales values over £500.

Watch What You're Selling

It's important to assess how well something has sold, how many buyers have contacted you and whether the sale has been worthwhile. Whilst you may never sell the same item twice, it helps to know the best places to sell, what sells quickly and slowly, when you should sell specific items, and for how much. The following section provides lots of advice on how you can generate your own market research for the future.

Watch Your eBay Auctions

During the auction of an item you're selling, you can see how many people are watching your auction. Many of these people may place bids during the last few minutes of the auction. You can also watch the bids to see who is bidding and whether they have automatic bids. An automatic bid will be placed after someone else has bid and will usually raise the bid by a few pounds. Automatic bids are set with a specific maximum value and are often useful for fast bidding during the last few minutes of an auction.

Did You Know?

eBay can automatically email alerts to you concerning the bid status of an auctioned item.

Add a Counter to eBay

Setting up an eBay listing was covered earlier in this chapter including the addition of a counter using the advanced settings when creating a listing. The counter shows how many people have opened the web page with details of the item you are selling (unlike the watch figure where buyers have to select to watch your item). One person may open the page several times and each time is counted. The counter can be displayed on the page or hidden, but in both cases it gives you some information on the interest in your item.

Watch Other Auctions

Whilst your eBay auction is running, keep searching for similar items that are on eBay. You may find your item is more expensive than other similar items, or another item is better described and offers better value for money. If this is the case, you may want to edit your eBay listing.

Classified Feedback

It's not always so easy to gauge the success of a classified advertisement on some of the websites we've mentioned in this chapter. If the classified advertisement is on a forum, you can view and answer people's questions, but other types of classifieds may not offer much in the way of feedback. All you can do is look at similar items and make sure you have the competitive edge, for example, by offering it more cheaply or with more extras.

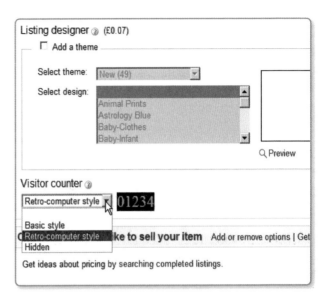

Above: Adding a counter to a listing helps to monitor the number of people who visit the web page for your item. This is different to the number of people watching the item.

Above: Items on eBay can be watched to monitor bids throughout the period of an auction.

Become a Pro Internet Seller

Professional Selling Options

There are a number of approaches to selling on a professional level via the internet, ranging from using someone else's website or a third party such as eBay or Amazon, to creating and managing your own website. The following section outlines the different options.

Selling Websites

Websites ranging from eBay and Amazon to general and specialized classifieds can all be used to sell items. eBay and Amazon can be customized to help you represent yourself in a professional capacity, and this is covered in greater detail in this chapter. Websites featuring classified advertising were covered in the previous chapter.

Made-to-order Items

There are a number of websites that can sell personalized and customized products, such as stickers, cards, clothing and books, which are manufactured for you and sold on your behalf. In some cases, the products are sold through the manufacturer's website and you receive a commission on each sale. Personalized product websites such as Café Press offer a variety of selling schemes and incentives to help sell anything from a fridge magnet to a T-shirt sporting your own design.

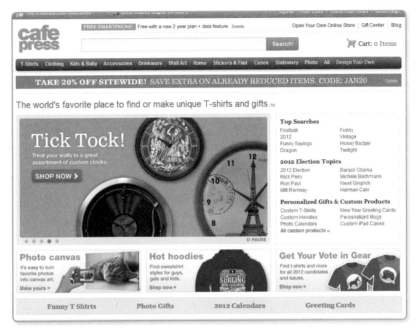

Above: Café Press offers a selling platform for customized designs that can be printed on to stickers, clothing and books.

Make Your Own Shop

Creating your own website to sell items requires a reasonable level of technical knowledge, especially if you want a fully automated and controlled system. However, you can start with a straightforward website that requires customers to contact you if they want to place an order. Buyers often feel more secure if they can telephone or send an email. Chapter five (Make a Website) covers all you need to know about creating your own website.

Hot Tip

Chapter six (Other Money-making Ideas) covers details on writing your own book and selling it on the internet.

E-commerce

Selling on a professional and large scale often requires some degree of automation, especially if sales are worldwide. Whilst selling websites such as Amazon and eBay offer these solutions, if you want to manage this for yourself, then take a look at what the world of e-commerce can offer. There are specialists who can develop a website to handle sales, or software that can be purchased to help create a shop front for a website and automatically handle orders. The main elements of e-commerce include the following:

Stock: A database is often used to record stock levels and prices, which can then be used to calculate the total cost of an order and make sure stock is available.

Shopping cart: A reliable method of adding one or more products to purchase whilst browsing through the website. This is also known as a shopping basket.

	Qty.	Product(s)	Each	Total
Remove Item ▷	1	Canon Lens Hood -	£17.99	£17.99
Remove Item ▷	1	Ring LED Cyba Lite	£1.49	£2.99
Remove Item ▷	1	iPad Smooth (TPU) Soft Gel Case	£2.99	£1.49
Remove Item ▷	1	Panasonic Zinc Carbon - PP3 (6F22) 9V -	£1.39	£1.39
Remove All ▷				Sub-Total: £23.86
Go Back ◁		Update Cart ▷		Checkout ▷

Above: A shopping basket is a useful e-commerce feature that enables customers to browse through your website and add multiple purchases before paying for all of them together.

Checkout: A secure method of paying for all the goods ordered.

Log in: Many websites with e-commerce require customers to log in with a username and password, which allows their personal details to be stored (useful for future purchases). This provides additional security methods to safeguard against fraud.

Business on eBay

A registered business can become an eBay member and sell its goods at auction or through classified ads. eBay can help to promote a business and reduced fees are often applicable. The following section outlines what's involved in registering as a business with eBay and what the benefits are.

Register a Business With eBay

When registering as an eBay member, there is the option to register as a business. Whilst the process of registering as a business or private individual is roughly the same, registering as a business has the advantage of being able to add your business name and contact details to your account.

Who Qualifies as a Business?
eBay recommends if you do any of the following types of buying and selling you should be registered as a business with them:

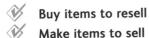 **Buy items to resell**

Make items to sell

Regularly sell a large volume of goods

Sell new items

Sell items for other people

Above: Changing an eBay account from private to business is straightforward through 'Personal information' on the 'Account' tab of 'My eBay'.

Did You Know?

If you already have a non-business account with eBay, you can convert this to a business account, but you can't change it back.

eBay and Tax

In some countries, there are tax implications of operating through eBay on a large scale as a private individual and avoiding paying tax on your profits. If you are running a business, this should be declared to the Inland Revenue (HMRC, the IRS or your country's equivalent). This is covered in greater detail in chapter seven (Legal Issues).

Benefits of a Business on eBay

Operating as a registered business does have several benefits, including the following:

 Business name promotion: A business can display its name in all communications with its buyers, including invoices and emails. This will help to promote the business and set it apart from non-business eBay members.

☑ **VAT back**: If your business is VAT registered, you can claim the VAT back in some countries or receive invoices net of VAT, but this is only usually possible if you are registered as a business member with eBay.

☑ **Discount fees**: Some fees are discounted for eBay members registered as businesses, especially if other business-related packages are used (see later in this chapter for more details).

☑ **PowerSeller and top-rated**: You can only gain respectable seller ratings, such as becoming a PowerSeller or top-rated seller, if you are registered as a business member with eBay.

> **Hot Tip**
>
> If you use your eBay account to sell private and business items, then you can create two accounts to separate the different types.

☑ **Contact details**: Business sellers can display their full contact details in each of their listings, which allows buyers to telephone or email them.

☑ **Offset expenses**: For taxation purposes, any fees incurred through the sale of items can be counted as expenses and offset against tax.

Business Costs on eBay

Some of the fees charged by eBay are cheaper if you are registered as a business, but others are more expensive. However, some fees are cheaper still if you use other business-related features from eBay that require a monthly subscription (covered later in this chapter). The following list outlines some of the fees to expect if you are registered as a business with eBay:

☑ **Insertion fees**: This is similar to selling an item as a private individual, with costs ranging from free to as much as £1.30 or $2, depending on the starting price.

Classified ads such as property are charged at standard rates (property listings cost £35 in the UK).

 Fixed-price listing: If an item is listed with a fixed price, then an insertion fee costs between 20p and 40p, but can be cheaper if you have an eBay shop (see later in this chapter).

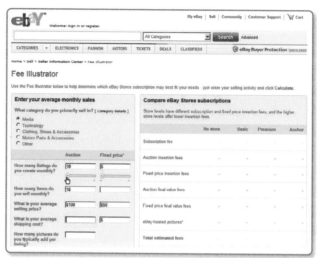

Above: eBay includes a Fee Illustrator to help estimate the fees generated on numerous sales.

 Reserve price: Charged at 1–3% of the reserve price, but often up to a specific maximum amount. A reserve price on property is in most cases charged at a flat rate.

 Final value: Ranges from 3–12%, depending on the category of the item and the country in which you are registered with eBay.

Sample Fees

If a UK eBay member that is registered as a business lists a pair of shoes with a starting price of 99p and sells them for £25, then the fees incurred include a 10p listing fee and 12% of the final value (£3). If the same shoes were sold with a reserve price of £20, then the listing fee would have been 50p (based on the reserve price), the reserve price fee would have been 60p and the final value fee would still be £3 (12% of the final value). So in this case, adding a reserve fee increases costs by £1.

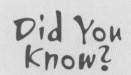

Did You Know?

Fees vary between the different countries in which eBay is hosted.

eBay Scores

Successful selling through eBay is all down to ratings in the form of positive feedback from buyers. This can be best achieved by gaining a good reputation for being a reliable and honest seller. All eBay members who buy and sell are rated to help establish their reliability and honesty. The following pages outline how you are assessed and how a good rating will result in more sales.

Ratings and Feedback

One of the most important aspects of eBay that will help give confidence to potential buyers and reassure them of your reliability is to maintain good ratings and feedback. This can only be built up over time as you buy and sell more and more items.

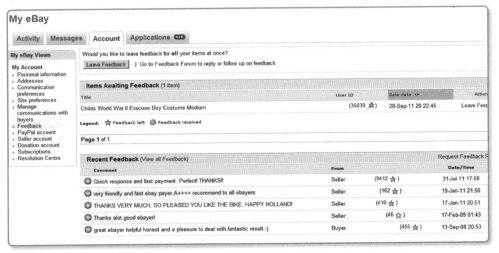

Above: You can view the finer details of feedback from buyers and sellers you've done business with to help assess your ratings.

Feedback Profile

Whenever you buy or sell something, eBay requests you to leave feedback about the transaction that assesses your experience with the buyer or seller. At the same time, the buyer or seller (trading partner) is asked to leave feedback about you. Over time, eBay members will develop a Feedback Profile, which is based on the comments and ratings left by other members.

Feedback Score

This is one of the most important parts of an eBay member's Feedback Profile. It's the number in brackets next to a member's user ID and it's also located at the top of the member's Feedback Profile. The Feedback Score is calculated according to ratings given by the buyers and sellers you do business with. A positive rating earns one point, a neutral rating earns no points and a negative rating deducts one point.

Other Feedback Data

Whilst the Feedback Score in brackets is useful, there are other values and symbols to look out for, including the following:

 Percentage: This is the percentage of positive ratings left by eBay members in the last year. The percentage is calculated by dividing the number of positive ratings by the total number of ratings (positive and negative).

Recent feedback ratings: This can be viewed by looking at an eBay member's profile and clicking on a button labelled 'See all feedback'. The total number of positive, neutral and negative feedback ratings the member has received are listed over the last one, six and 12 months.

Recent Feedback ratings (last 12 months)	?		
	1 month	6 months	12 months
Positive	2	5	11
Neutral	0	0	0
Negative	0	0	0

Above: The feedback ratings received in the last one to 12 months for an eBay member can help potential buyers and sellers decide whether to do business.

 Comments: Look at the Feedback Profile of an eBay member and you can see the comments posted by other members who have bought or sold from them.

Right: When an item is purchased from an eBay member, the buyer can leave anonymous Detailed Seller Ratings (DSR) concerning the accuracy of description, the seller's communication, speed of dispatch and postage costs.

DSR

Detailed Seller Ratings (DSR) are anonymous ratings given by buyers. There are four categories relating to the accuracy of description, the seller's communication, speed of dispatch and postage costs with star ratings out of five. DSRs are essential for professional sellers who want to increase their profile through eBay (see the next section).

eBay PowerSeller and Top-rated Sellers

eBay offers the facilities to become a professional seller and ensure potential buyers are frequently looking at what you have to offer. If you're interested in expanding or moving an existing high-street business on to the internet, or would like to see if selling on eBay could be turned into a full-time occupation, the following pages provide information on eBay's usefulness to professional selling.

Feedback earned for transactions on eBay			View your eBay My World page
Positive Feedback: 99.9%	**Detailed Seller Ratings** (last 12 months)		⑦
Feedback score: 3999	Criteria	Average rating	Number of ratings
[How is Feedback calculated?]	Item as described	★★★★★	622
	Communication	★★★★★	616
	Dispatch time	★★★★★	616
	Postage and packaging charges	★★★★★	615

Left: A number of criteria need to be met to become a PowerSeller, including high DSRs.

eBay PowerSeller

An eBay PowerSeller is an automatic classification based on a high level of positive feedback from buyers, a specific minimum amount of annual sales and other criteria. Being rated as a PowerSeller provides buyers with greater confidence and this rating is displayed against every listing you have (plus it's displayed alongside your profile). The following list of criteria entitles an eBay member to become classified as a PowerSeller (values may differ in some countries):

 90 days business seller: To become a PowerSeller, you must be registered with eBay for at least 90 days and also be registered as a business seller.

 Pay your bills: Payments for fees must be made on time.

✅ **Positive feedback**: Over the last year, feedback needs to be at least 98% positive.

✅ **Sales**: A specific minimum sales volume over one year to buyers in your country. In the UK this is currently £2000 and in the USA this is $3000.

✅ **Detailed Seller Ratings**: Receive at least a 4.60 average across all four DSR categories with no more than 1% of transactions with low DSRs (1s or 2s) on item as described, and a maximum of 2% of low DSRs on communication, dispatch time and postage costs.

✅ **Complaints and cases**: For all transactions, you must have no more than 1% of transactions resulting in an opened eBay Buyer Protection and PayPal Buyer Protection case, plus no more than 0.3% of transactions resulting in closed cases without a resolution.

PowerSeller Benefits

PowerSeller status entitles you to priority customer support, promotional offers, discounted postage costs in some countries and involvement with eBay promotions and research. The key to becoming a PowerSeller, aside from maintaining a level of sales, is to keep your customers happy. Honesty pays and providing your customers are happy in their dealings with you, they will keep your ratings high enough to ensure you remain a PowerSeller.

PowerSeller to Top-rated

Once you have become established as a PowerSeller, you can move up to becoming a top-rated seller. This is displayed as a yellow rosette against all items you sell and helps to give you a competitive edge. Your items in some cases receive a better placing in search results and you're entitled to discounts on final value fees. However, the criteria for top-rated seller status are stricter than those required of a PowerSeller, with lower allowances for negative DSRs.

Above: PowerSellers with a top-rated award have preferential listings in search results and are displayed with a 'Top-rated seller' rosette.

eBay Shops and Stores

An eBay shop or store provides the advantage of displaying all the items you are selling on eBay and keeping in contact with your regular buyers. You can have your own eBay-related website address, such as www.stores.ebay.co.uk/myshop, and access to sales tools and data. There are three types of eBay shop, which are fully outlined in the following section.

Above: Running an eBay shop allows all your products to be featured in one place. Illston and Robson are manufacturers of airline couplings, ball joints and linkages and use an eBay shop to list around 50 products.

Types of eBay shop

There are three different types of eBay shop, which are as follows:

 Basic Shop/Store: This is suitable for anyone registered with eBay as a business or private individual with a PayPal account. Monthly fees cost £14.99 in the UK and $15.95 in the USA with reduced insertion fees and discounted final value fees.

 Featured/Premium Shop/Store: In some countries, this is only available for registered business sellers on eBay. A PayPal account is required and a minimum average Detailed Seller Rating (DSR) over 12 months is stipulated in all four categories. With cheaper insertion fees than a basic shop/store and also discounts on other fees, the only fee that is greater is the monthly subscription, which at present is £49.99 in the UK and $49.95 in the USA (different discounts apply between the two countries).

Anchor Shop/Store: The same criteria for a Featured Shop apply to an Anchor Shop, but the average DSR must be higher. Consequently, the rewards for achieving this status are greater with larger discounts on fees, but also a higher monthly subscription of £349.99 in the UK and $299.95 in the USA.

What's the Difference?

There are several differences between the three eBay shops or stores, which reflect the amount you can sell, the level of promotion and the selling tools and analysis provided by eBay. The following helps to summarize some of the main differences and benefits:

 Sales tools: Sales software tools such as Selling Manager Pro are provided for free with Featured/Premium and Anchor Shops/Stores. This online tool helps to create listings and manage

Above: The main page for eBay stores provides greater promotion for Anchor Shops, which pay the greatest monthly subscription fees.

sales and stock. Other free tools allow discounts to be applied and managed online (the more expensive the subscription, the greater the number of items that can be discounted).

 Custom pages: These pages can help to customize your shop and provide space to display information. The number of pages provided varies according to the type of shop/store and the country (five to 15 in the UK, but 15 in the USA).

 Space for images: Online storage space for logos and custom page images is provided for free with an increasing amount according to the type of eBay shop/store.

 Email marketing: Customized emails can be sent to customers. The amount of emails that can be sent ranges between 1000 and 10,000, depending on the type of eBay shop/store.

Promotion on http://stores.ebay: The main web page for eBay shops includes your shop details, depending on the type of shop you have. Featured shops have a rotational listing in the bottom middle of the screen. Anchor Shops have a similar promotion (logo) in the centre of the page.

Success Story

Amanda O'Brien has become a successful PowerSeller on eBay and discovered some of the most effective methods of selling on a large scale. One product she has successfully sold is a simple teeth-whitening kit, which she bought wholesale for £3.75 per kit, then sold for £12.99 with £2.25 postage, resulting in a profit (when you take off the various eBay and PayPal fees) of £8.26 per sale. Through careful placement and favourable ratings within eBay, Amanda managed to achieve average sales of eight kits per day and moved her formula on to other products, resulting in £2500 profit per week. She puts her success down to careful research, sourcing products at the right price from wholesalers and always using her own proven strategies for every new product she sources and sells.

Above: Amanda O'Brien has discovered several methods for successfully selling on eBay.

Buy the Books

The story and secrets behind Amada O'Brien's eBay success can now be discovered in a number of books she has written, which are available through her websites including www.powersellerprofiteer.co.uk and www.powersellerpod.com. These books are home-study courses, designed to guide you through successful selling on eBay.

Above: Amanda O'Brien has written a number of books outlining how to succeed through selling on eBay. This one is available for £67 through www.powersellerprofiteer.co.uk.

eBay Trading Assistants

If you're keen to continue selling items on eBay, but don't want to get involved in the logistics of buying or sourcing more stock, then one solution is to sell other people's goods and become an eBay Trading Assistant. It's free to become an eBay Trading Assistant, but there are some rules. The following section outlines what's involved.

Trading Assistant Criteria

To become an eBay Trading Assistant, there are certain criteria you must satisfy, which vary between countries, but usually concern the following:

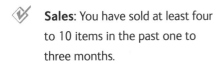 **Sales:** You have sold at least four to 10 items in the past one to three months.

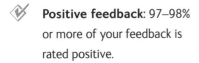 **Positive feedback:** 97–98% or more of your feedback is rated positive.

Pay your bills: Your eBay account is in good order and you have paid your fees on time.

It's also useful to have at least one drop-off location for people to deliver items to you. However, you can also offer a collection service and charge a fee for this (including a nationwide collection using a courier such as DHL).

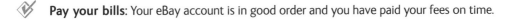

Click to Become a Trading Assistant

If you meet the aforementioned criteria to become a Trading Assistant, then you can change a private account to a business account – an eBay member registered as a business can choose to become a Trading Assistant. After logging into your eBay account, click on My eBay at the top of the screen and select Summary. Click on the Account tab on the left side of the screen and choose Personal Information from the left. Look for your Account Type and click on Edit. A new screen will appear where you can choose Business Account. You will then need to choose some Trading Assistant details.

Trading Assistant settings

After logging into eBay and viewing your Account (see previous section for instructions), select Create/Edit Your Profile down the left side of the screen. You can then create a profile in the Trading Assistant Directory, stating what you sell, your fees, terms, contact information and drop-off and collection details. You can create more than one profile in the Trading Assistant directory, which is useful if you have several drop-off locations.

Hot Tip

Before becoming a Trading Assistant, find other Trading Assistants in your area and see what they offer.

Trading Assistant Fees

eBay charges the standard insertion, final value and other fees for Trading Assistants to sell items in the same manner as private individuals and registered businesses. It is up to the Trading Assistant to decide what fees they want to charge to sell items and make their money. Some Trading Assistants charge an initial minimum fee, such as £5 or $5 to sell items up to a specific amount and £10 or $10 to sell items over this amount. They then charge a percentage of the selling price if the item sells. Other Trading Assistants just charge a percentage of the selling price (the final value).

Logistics

The idea of selling other people's goods and charging a commission may sound tempting, but if you are interested, it's worthwhile spending time looking into the following issues:

- ☑ **Storage**: You may need a large area to store your items, especially if you intend to have a large turnover. If you have to pay for storage and insurance, this has to be accounted for and covered in the commission you charge.

- ☑ **Unsaleable items**: Decide upon a policy for items that will not sell. Does the supplier collect them? And what happens if they don't collect them? Should they, if possible, be donated to charity or disposed of? Remember you may have to pay to dispose of items.

Agree a price: What happens if you recommend a price for an item and the supplier disagrees? Similarly, if a supplier wants a minimum amount for an item, but you feel this is unreasonable, you must have a policy in place to resolve this dispute.

 Minimum value: Most Trading Assistants do not sell items that are valued at less than £50. The time involved in photographing, listing and posting such an item isn't worth the profit you will make as a Trading Assistant.

Trading Assistant Success Story

Michael Woodhouse runs DJ Mike's eBay Shop, which sells people's unwanted items. He used to have a high-street shop in the centre of Hull where people could drop off items and collect things that hadn't sold, but has since cut down on his expenditure and closed the shop in favour of cheaper storage premises. Being an eBay member since 2003, Michael has sold a wide variety of items for people, ranging from a Fisher Price play set to a Brother knitting machine. With a 30% commission charge on the sale price (final value), or 20% if the sale price exceeds £1000, the one problem he has found is disposing of items that don't sell. Consequently, Michael states on his Trading Assistant Directory profile that, 'Any unsold items not collected after 90 days will be sold at a lower price or donated to charity at our discretion'.

Above: Michael Woodhouse is an eBay Trading Assistant, helping others to sell their unwanted goods.

Payment: Find the cheapest and easiest way to pay your suppliers and receive payments. Whilst PayPal must be offered for selling items, it incurs a fee for every payment you receive and if you pay a supplier, they are also charged a fee. Some Trading Assistants pay their suppliers by cheque or a bank payment (known as BACS – Bankers Automated Clearing Service).

> # Hot Tip
>
> **If you are interested in becoming a Trading Assistant, but are unsure of how to proceed, look at what other Trading Assistants offer on eBay.**

Cheaper Overheads on the Internet

Since Michael Woodhouse has moved from his high-street premises to a business unit, his overheads have been reduced by a massive 70%. He has also found the volume of trade (that is, people bringing their unwanted items to him to sell) has not been affected by not having a high-street location.

Trading Assistant to Trading Post

If an eBay business operating as a Trading Assistant becomes big and successful, then it can move up to being a Trading Post, which sometimes provides priority placement in search results. Trading Posts are displayed with a special icon next to their user ID. However, there are a few rules that must be adhered to, which include the following:

 Staffed drop-off: You must have a staffed drop-off location with regular opening hours.

 Feedback: A feedback score of 500 or higher is required.

- ☑ **Positive feedback:** A 98% or higher positive feedback score is essential.

- ☑ **Sales:** eBay sales must be at least £15,000 per month in the UK and vary in other countries.

Hot Tip

A Trading Post is automatically awarded to a Trading Assistant when they meet the stated criteria.

Success Story – Trading Assistant Becomes Marketing Specialist

Alistair Hague is behind Sheffield-based Alchemistic Ltd, which has taken the role of Trading Assistant to a professional level (see www.alchemistic.co.uk). The company offers bespoke eBay marketing services for businesses across the world, providing everything from a pricing strategy and photography to handling payments and returns. At the time of viewing, Alchemistic was selling camping equipment (including seconds), Zippo lighters, clothing and umbrellas and more. Consequently, this eBay seller is also a PowerSeller with over 3000 ratings in the last 12 months.

Above: Sheffield-based Alchemistic has taken the role of eBay Trading Assistant to a professional level through its own website.

Small-scale selling on Amazon

Amazon originally became known as an online bookseller, but has evolved into selling a wide range of goods on behalf of businesses and private individuals. In the UK, Amazon Marketplace enables you to sell new, used, collectible and refurbished items alongside their new ones. In the USA and elsewhere in the world, there are equivalent small-scale selling services through Amazon.

Amazon Rules

There are a number of rules and regulations to adhere to when selling on a small scale through Amazon. These include the following for the UK (similar rules apply to other countries):

- **No auction**: Amazon Marketplace and equivalent Amazon selling services are not auctions. You have to set a fixed price for an item and may be competing with other sellers who offer cheaper prices and delivery methods.

- **Quick delivery**: Amazon notifies you by email when one of your items is bought. You must dispatch the goods within two days of receiving this email.

✓ **Low volume**: In the UK, you are allowed to sell a maximum of 33 items per month on Amazon Marketplace and in the USA the limit is 40. If you want to sell more than this quota, you may want to look at some of the professional selling services, such as becoming a Pro-Merchant Seller, which is covered later in this chapter.

✓ **Already listed**: An item must already be listed for sale in Amazon. You cannot add an item that is not already listed unless you become a Pro-Merchant Seller, which is covered later in this chapter.

✓ **Prohibited**: You cannot sell mobile phones, subscriptions to publications, tobacco, alcohol, adult toys, gift cards and certificates, prescription medication, photo processing or guns and ammunition on Amazon Marketplace.

Hot Tip

Amazon Marketplace is a useful way of selling items on the internet on a small scale and avoids the hassle of handling credit and debit card payments because Amazon does this for you.

Amazon Marketplace Fees

Amazon Marketplace does not charge to list an item, but it does charge the following once an item has been purchased:

✓ **Completion fee**: A small fee is charged for the completed sale of an item. At present, this is 86p in the UK and $0.99 in the USA.

✓ **Closing fee**: A percentage of the sale price is charged as a fee. This varies according to the category of the item and the country in which Amazon is based. Fees range from as little as 6% up to 25%. As a general rule, computer equipment and electrical goods carry the cheapest fees, whereas clothes and food demand a higher percentage.

 Delivery charge fee: There is a range of fees applicable to the delivery charge (called variable closing fees). Some are free, whereas others start at a specific amount and others are charged according to weight.

VAT Back

Amazon Marketplace in the UK and Europe charges 15% VAT (value added tax) on its fees, so if you run a VAT-registered business, this can be claimed back. For example, if you sell a book for £100, Amazon Marketplace will charge 86p to complete the sale of which you can claim back 13p. It will also charge £17.25 commission (17.25%) and you will be able to claim back £2.25. Consequently, the fees for the sale of the book will come to £15.73 if you can claim the VAT back.

Did You Know?

You get a store-front website address after setting up an account with Amazon Marketplace. The address begins with www.amazon.co.uk/shops/ followed by your Marketplace name.

Sell on Amazon Marketplace

Before selling items through Amazon Marketplace or the equivalent Amazon small-scale selling service for your country, you will need the following information:

Above: Amazon Marketplace is a good starting point for anyone wanting to sell a few items each month.

✔ **Credit card**: Credit card details are held by Amazon in case payment is required to cover the cost of a subscription fee.

✔ **Telephone number**: A suitable number where Amazon Marketplace can contact you if required.

✔ **Bank account details**: Amazon Marketplace will make payments to this account. It can pay into UK, Austrian, French, German and US bank accounts.

✔ **VAT number**: If you have a VAT-registered business, Amazon Marketplace will need to know your VAT number to help ensure your fees are VAT free.

E-mail address: A large amount of correspondence from Amazon Marketplace is conducted via email, including messages from customers and potential buyers.

Register with Amazon

If you already have an account with Amazon, then you can log in with this account at www.amazon.co.uk for the UK, www.amazon.com for the USA (other countries that Amazon sells in include Canada, China, Japan and several European countries). If you haven't got an account with Amazon, then you can create one by visiting the relevant Amazon website. However, you can also proceed with selling an item on Amazon Marketplace without having to log in first (see later in this chapter for steps on selling on Amazon Marketplace), but you will still need to create an account.

Check What's Selling

Before you proceed with selling an item through Amazon, it's worthwhile conducting some market research first. Visit Amazon's website and search for the item you want to sell (enter its details in the search box near the top of the screen). If any results appear, select them to see the prices and postage costs. Also, check the text that describes the items for sale to get ideas for how you can write your own text. These items are your competition and you need to think about how potential customers are going to choose your item over everyone else's.

Above: Before selling an item through Amazon Marketplace, have a look to see if it is already being sold and what the price range is.

Hot Tip

Do not copy another seller's description to use for selling the same item yourself. Try to find a better way of wording your own description.

Step-by-step Small-scale Selling on Amazon

1. **Start selling**: When you're ready to sell something on Amazon, visit Amazon's website, scroll down to the bottom of the screen and select 'Sell on Amazon' (below the heading 'Make Money with Us'). The next page to appear is titled 'Sell on Amazon'. Under the section called 'Sell a little' or 'Sell a lot', click on the 'Start selling' button.

Above: Amazon Marketplace provides straightforward step-by-step procedures to selling an item online.

Above: Once you have found a listing for the item you want to sell, click on the 'Sell yours here' button.

2. **Find the item**: Under the section called Step 1, there will be a drop-down box containing product categories for your item. Select one from the list, then type its name into the box to the right. If you are selling a book and know its ISBN, a product with a Universal Product Code (UPC), or something with an Amazon Standard Identification Number (ASIN), then this can be entered on this page. In all cases, click on the 'Start selling' button.

3. **Sell yours here**: A list of suitable products that match your search will be listed on the screen (less if you entered a code for it). If your item is listed, click on the relevant 'Sell yours here' button to the right of the listed item. If you are unsure it's the correct item, click on it to see further details.

4. **Condition**: Once you have clicked on the 'Sell yours here' button, the item will be displayed on the screen and you now have the opportunity to describe its condition by selecting a choice from a drop-down list. You can also add a note in the box below to help further describe its condition. Click on the 'Continue' button near the bottom of the screen to proceed to the next step.

Above: Choose a suitable description for the condition of the item you're selling. There's also a separate box where you can further describe the item's condition.

5. **Price**: Enter the price you want for the item, taking into account the fees that Amazon will take from this amount. If you have a few of the same item to sell, change the number in the quantity box. Finally, decide what delivery options you want to offer, then click on the 'Continue' button. If you have not logged into Amazon, you will have to do this now.

6. **Account details**: If you haven't sold anything on Amazon Marketplace before, you will now be able to enter a display name that buyers will see. This is a unique name, so you may find many obvious names have already been used (click on 'Check availability' to see if a name has been used). You may also need to add your credit card details.

Hot Tip

Only certain items can be sold on Amazon according to a specific number of categories (see the next section for a wider range).

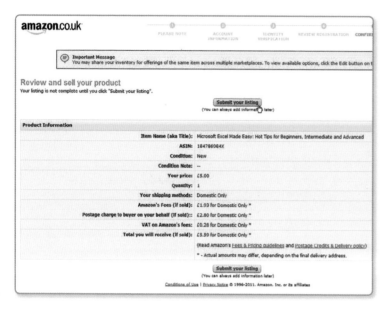

7. **Verify identity**: Your identity may need verifying. If this is the case, make sure the correct phone number is displayed, then click on the button to receive a phone call. A four digit PIN will be displayed on the screen. When your telephone rings, answer it and type or say the PIN when prompted. If this is confirmed, put the phone down and click on the 'Register and continue' button.

Above: A summary of the item you want to sell and how much Amazon Marketplace will charge is displayed on screen before you submit the listing. Even at this stage you can click on the 'Edit' button and cancel the listing.

8. **Submit listing**: After a few seconds, Amazon Marketplace will display a summary of what you are selling, how much it will charge and what the postage costs are. If you are happy to proceed, click on the 'Submit your listing' button. The listing can be edited at a later date or can be edited now by clicking on the 'Edit' button near the top right of the screen (this also enables you to cancel the listing).

Did You Know?

When describing the condition of an item you are selling through Amazon Marketplace, you can write up to 2000 characters.

Large-scale Selling Through Amazon

Whilst Amazon Marketplace and equivalent Amazon small-scale selling features are useful for anyone wanting to sell a few items, if you want to list a large amount of goods for sale, you will need to become a professional seller with Amazon. This is also essential for some types of goods, such as beauty products in the USA.

Professional Eligibility

Operating a Professional Seller's account on Amazon (also called a Pro-Merchant account) requires you to adhere to the following criteria:

- **Email**: an email address is required to receive notification of new purchases.

- **Quick dispatch**: Purchased items must be dispatched within a specific number of days. In the UK this is currently two working days.

- **Seller rating**: Buyers can rate your performance as a seller and your rating must remain strong (above three out of five).

- **Inventory-loading tools**: The Pro-Merchant account includes tools to upload data concerning stock. However, Amazon requires the data to be in a tab-delimited form, which can be created in a spreadsheet or database.

Professional Seller Fees

The following fees are charged by Amazon for a Professional Seller (Pro-Merchant) account:

Monthly subscription: A monthly fee of £25+VAT is charged in the UK (VAT is charged at a European-wide rate of 15%, so the total fee comes to £28.75) and $39.99 in the USA.

No closing fees: Unlike an Amazon Marketplace account, there are no closing fees with a Professional or Pro-Merchant account, so Amazon does not charge you a fixed fee for selling something.

Sales commission: Amazon charges between 6 and 25% (plus VAT at 15% in the UK) for selling items. In some cases (for example, DVDs in the UK), Amazon charges from a range of fixed fees.

Postage: Known as a variable closing fee, Amazon charges from a range of fixed prices relating to the postage costs. Some items are not charged, but the postage cost is added to the sale price and a percentage taken in the sales commission charge.

Pro or Not?

At first, it may seem difficult to understand why someone would want to open a Professional Seller's account on Amazon. The following list outlines some of the benefits:

 Large scale: If you are involved in selling around 40 or more items per month, this helps to justify the monthly subscription fee, which then becomes cheaper than paying individual closing fees.

 Five European Marketplaces: Amazon Europe has five Marketplaces and goods can be sold through all of these. Similar continent and worldwide markets are available in other areas of the world.

 All categories: A Marketplace or individual account can only list goods for sale in the most popular categories, whereas a Pro-Merchant or Professional Seller account allows goods to be listed in all categories.

 1-click purchasing: Amazon's famous 1-click online purchasing can be applied to your goods for sale.

 New products: You can add new products to Amazon.

 Analysis: You can view order reports, inventory and other data to assess the performance of your business through Amazon.

Professional Precautions

Becoming a professional seller on the internet is often not an easy decision to make. You can't simply advertise some goods and worry about acquiring them if the orders start to flood in. Similarly, you may not want to spend a fortune on stock if it isn't going to sell. The following pages provide some useful guidelines when considering to become a professional seller on the internet.

Market Research

The most important point of a business is to know your market and have a clear understanding of what sells and how much money you can make. Whether you are selling hand-knitted scarves or buying and selling unwanted stock, you need to know the following facts and figures:

Competition and prices: Who else is selling the goods you want to sell and how much do they cost?

Your customers: Do you know where your customers are located and how they will find you? Can you be sure there are any customers for the goods you want to sell?

Competitive edge: Can you be sure customers will buy from you and not another supplier? What can you offer them that will give you the advantage and persuade customers to buy from you?

Where to sell: Do you know where most people currently buy the goods you intend to sell?

Mark-up and profit: Make sure you know how much profit can be made from the sale of your goods and have a clear understanding of all the costs involved, ranging from internet sales fees to postage and packing. A good businessperson has these figures memorized.

eBay and Amazon Data

The large internet selling websites such as eBay and Amazon often have information available concerning the sale of particular goods. A search on eBay for completed listings will reveal a lot of useful information that is available for free. In other cases, you may need to subscribe to access this information.

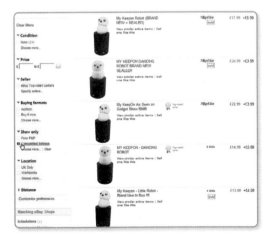

Right: Looking for completed listings on eBay helps to determine what people are willing to pay for a particular product.

Specialist Websites and Sellers

There are lots of specialist websites that cater for a particular interest, which may apply to the goods you are trying to sell and can help to ease you into the market without the need for huge investment. These range from enthusiasts' own websites to official clubs and associations.

Clubs and Associations

Whether it's a local camera club, classic car club or official association for a particular breed of dog, specialist websites are generally visited by people who have an interest in a specific subject. If this subject relates to the goods you want to sell, you've found some potential customers. It's worthwhile contacting such organizations to see how many active members they have and whether they are willing to take advertising or offers from you. A group buy, for instance, may help to launch a product and guarantee a minimum turnover.

Offer Commission

Building up a network of reliable on-sellers or agents may be one solution to selling your goods. This could be as simple as a selection of enthusiasts with their own websites or several eBay members who want to try selling.

Make It, Sell It

It's one of the oldest and most traditional ways of making money. Whether it's making your own jam from the strawberries in your garden and selling them at the local market, or selling your own paintings, this is one area of making money on the internet that most people find the easiest to understand and try. There are plenty of useful websites and selling services to help you sell such goods, ranging from craft sites such as www.etsy.com to general selling sites like eBay and Amazon.

Hot Tip

Website www.folksy.com sells British-made craft, ranging from clothes and greetings cards to wedding accessories and bookcases with listing fees at 22p and commission on sales at 5%+VAT.

Migrating to the Internet

If you already run a high-street shop or a similar business that buys and sells, you may be contemplating moving all or part of your business on to the internet. But how can you be sure it will be successful? The following pages outline some of the pros and cons to consider.

Planning Change

Many businesses find their trade via the internet grows and often replaces more traditional methods of selling via the high street, local markets and mail order. The internet offers benefits such as lower overheads and more customers. In other cases, the costs incurred in non-internet selling and the growing number of customers who have moved to the internet can force a business into looking at the internet to make its money. In both cases, it's necessary to plan ahead and always be prepared to explore new markets.

Pros and Cons of the Internet

If you already run a high-street shop or similar business that receives little or no custom from the internet, there are several points to consider before deciding to move into this new market. These include many of the following general points:

 Specialist services: Selling goods on the internet incurs costs, just like a high-street business. Find out how much it will cost to sell your items on the internet, set up a website, take payments and use specialists who can increase business activity.

☑ **Competition**: Many businesses have found the internet provides a wider range of customers, but comes with fierce competition where price is often the only perceptible competitive edge.

☑ **Fraud**: Most businesses are already aware of the potential for fraud, but the internet carries a lot more risks. Most of these potential problems are discussed in chapter seven (Legal Issues).

☑ **Storage**: Whilst a high-street shop may have high overheads due to its location, you may still find you need some form of storage for goods, which incurs a cost.

Success Story of a Tools Seller

In 2010, Lee Ward was spending most of his weekends selling tools at auto jumbles, car shows and other events around the UK. He had a warehouse packed with stock, but has recently transferred his business activities to the internet. He runs an eBay shop as a top-rated seller of tools (UnitedTools2011) and other websites such as www.unitedtools.co.uk.

Above: Lee Ward sells tools through his eBay shop and a website, which he has found more successful than selling at trade and car shows.

With sales now exceeding the amount Lee could make from the weekend shows and storage costs reduced by a massive 70% by swapping the warehouse for several containers, Lee hasn't looked back.

Left: Lee Ward used to spend most of his weekends selling tools at car shows, but now relies on an eBay shop and other websites for customers.

The Logistics of Selling

Buying Stock

The bottom line of running a business that sells goods on the internet is making sure there's sufficient stock so that when an order is placed, the goods can be dispatched. Sounds simple? The following pages outline some of the disasters that can arise and how to plan to avoid them.

Acquisition

There are often several items that need to be purchased to be able to sell goods, even if it's just one specific product. These include the following:

Raw materials: If you are making a product, there may be a number of items required, such as materials or another product that is adapted.

Specialist services: Your product may need to be painted or finished by someone with specialist equipment.

Packaging: Both packaging for the product and packaging for delivery may be required.

Acquisition Logistics

Whether you are selling on goods that you've bought, adapting an existing product or making something from raw materials, the amount of organization required to ensure you have sufficient supplies can take up a lot of your time, especially if suppliers let you down. Consequently, you can never sit back and let the orders roll in. Always consider the following points:

> **Hot Tip**
>
> Many products are brand labelled. Providing you have a computer and printer, it's easy to brand the products you sell with your own logo and labelling.

Sourcing suppliers: Keep looking for reliable suppliers and work with your current suppliers to ensure they remain consistent and deliver on time.

Contingency plans: Are there other ways of sourcing the goods you are selling, even if it is more expensive? Such alternatives may be required at times, so seek out a few. This also applies to every aspect of your business, from buying stock to using a delivery service.

Acquisition Accounting

Keeping track of the stock you have bought is essential to ensure you can calculate whether or not you're making a profit. It's easy for stock to disappear or be wasted, especially packaging and small raw materials, so adopt some method of inventory, whether it's a list on a piece of paper, a spreadsheet, database or an accounting system.

Hot Tip

Flame Tree Publishing's book *Microsoft Excel Made Easy* contains information that can help with managing aspects of a business.

Methods for Buying Stock

Purchasing stock, whether raw materials or completed products, can be one of the biggest logistical problems of a business. Whilst the price needs to be low to maximize profit, the suppliers need to be reliable and these two issues often relate to each other. There are various approaches to sourcing your stock, which include the following:

- **Group buys and discounts**: Consider buying in bulk to receive greater discounts, or promising a minimum level of purchases over a specific period of time. Also, can you team up with others to buy in bulk?

- **Old raw materials**: If raw materials are required to make a product, consider sourcing this from old unwanted goods versus buying it new from a supplier.

- **Liquidated stock**: Several specialists buy and sell liquidated stock and are often interested in selling items in bulk. This type of stock can also be found at local auctions.

Above: Look at other markets for parts. This handmade tractor from Real Life Toys uses wheels and tyres from a full-sized ride-on tractor, fake engine parts from a car engine and a drainpipe for an exhaust pipe.

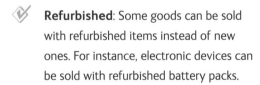
Refurbished: Some goods can be sold with refurbished items instead of new ones. For instance, electronic devices can be sold with refurbished battery packs.

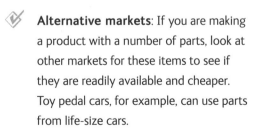
Alternative markets: If you are making a product with a number of parts, look at other markets for these items to see if they are readily available and cheaper. Toy pedal cars, for example, can use parts from life-size cars.

Hot Tip

Charity shops are a cheap source of sourcing items to sell on eBay and other online auctions. The goods are often sold at a reasonable price and bargains can often be found, which can be sold for more money elsewhere.

Stock Solutions

Selling goods doesn't necessarily mean you have to stock all of them so that they are ready to dispatch when an order is received. Instead, there are several other approaches to ensuring stock is available when sales are received. The following pages outline some of these answers.

Just in Time

The concept of manufacturing an item so that it is finished when the demand for it arises is known as the 'just in time' approach. Some mass-production car manufacturers have adopted this philosophy, which helps to reduce the cost of holding unused stock and also reduces storage space. On a smaller scale, a business selling goods can adopt a similar approach using its suppliers.

Buy When Needed

Some suppliers of goods can supply items at discounted prices, provided a minimum volume of goods is ordered over a given period. This helps to spread the cost of bulk buying and makes better use of your cashflow, as less of it will be tied up in stock that needs to be sold.

Hold Stock With the Supplier

If you have insufficient space to hold stock, you may find some suppliers can store it for you. Considering you are in a favourable position with a supplier because you have bought goods from them, there may be some scope to leave the stock with them, providing it isn't sold to someone else, leaving you short.

Fulfilment by Amazon

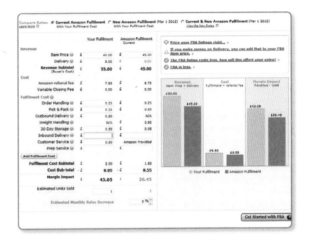

Amazon provides a worldwide service with its online shops called Fulfilment by Amazon, or FBA for short. In brief, it involves stocking the products you want to sell through Amazon at a fulfilment centre (an Amazon warehouse), so when an order is placed through Amazon, you let Amazon package and deliver the item(s). Customers see a Fulfilment by Amazon logo against any products you sell through this service, so whilst it's apparent the goods are from a third party, there is the reassurance that Amazon will deal with the order.

Above: Calculate the comparative costs of stocking and selling items yourself versus using Amazon Fulfilment to see which one is cheaper. This calculator is available online through Amazon.

What Can Be Sold Through FBA?

Amazon needs to be assured the goods you are selling through them are suitable, so they monitor your performance. Items ranging from books and music to toys, games, electronics and tools can be sold. There are some products that cannot be sold, however, including promotional CDs and DVDs, copied material (games, music, films) and products without relevant safety tags or codes. These rules and restrictions vary from country to country.

Sell to Other Countries

Depending on the country in which you reside, your products can be sold into other countries through FBA. For instance, UK sellers can have their products sold in up to 26 other European countries, ranging from Germany and France to Malta and Lithuania.

Discounted Delivery Costs

Delivery costs are based on Amazon's super-saver delivery rates and other standard methods of delivery. These types of delivery are offered with your product and as Amazon is packaging and posting your items (they are packed in Amazon-branded boxes), you can leave it to calculate the costings. In addition to relying on Amazon to use its standard delivery options, the tracking and messaging services are also available, which lets the customer know when a purchase has been dispatched and when it is due for delivery.

Who Can Join FBA?

You need to first become an Amazon seller to join the FBA scheme, whether it's a standard seller, business seller or Pro-Merchant. These types of seller are fully detailed in chapter two (Become a Pro Internet Seller), with information on how to join and what is involved in selling through Amazon.

Submitting Items for FBA

Any products you want to sell through Fulfilment by Amazon need to be listed in the standard way. These item listings then need to be converted to be fulfilled by Amazon. This is available online by editing the details of a listing. Once a listed item you are selling through Amazon has been converted to sell through FBA, it's removed from Amazon until it has been received and checked in at a fulfilment centre.

FBA Costs

There are no set-up fees to start selling through FBA, but there are a number of costs incurred, which include the following:

 Storage: Items for sale through FBA are charged storage costs, which are based on volume (cubic

feet or metres). Such costs are accrued on a monthly basis. Items that do not sell and are stored for more than one year incur higher storage costs.

Order handling: A handling charge is incurred in some cases; for example, where goods are sold through another sales channel other than the Amazon website for your country. In other cases, there is no handling charge.

Pick and pack: A small fee is incurred for someone to locate and pack the item. This varies and is dependent on factors such as the selling price.

Weight handling: A handling fee may be charged, which is based on the weight of the item.

The costs incurred in selling items through FBA can be cheaper than using your own premises to stock your items and spending your own time picking and packing. However, it's worth finding out the exact costs before committing.

Unsold Goods

If goods are not sold through FBA, they will incur a higher storage charge after one year, but can be returned to you for a fee, or disposed of for a smaller fee. At present, storage that exceeds one year is charged at £50 per cubic foot in the UK and $45 per cubic foot in the USA. Unsold goods that are returned to you incur a fee of £0.60–1.00 or $0.50, whilst disposal fees are half this amount.

Enquiries

Enquiries from potential buyers can take up a lot of your time, but they are essential in securing sales and ensuring your reputation and ratings remain high. There are several methods for dealing with customer enquiries and the following section outlines the most effective ones.

Dealing With Enquiries

The procedures involved in making a sale begin with a number of enquiries and questions, which hopefully lead to sales. This can be extremely time-consuming. There are many ways of dealing with these potential sales, all of which have advantages and disadvantages:

Above: Live chat services are a popular method of answering queries via your website, allowing you to deal with several customers at a time.

 Email: Answering enquiries via email enables you to allocate time to the task and it doesn't distract you from other activities. However, it can be time-consuming and it's often a slow method of closing a sale, as several emails have to travel back and forth.

 FAQ: A frequently asked questions section attached to your website or seller site can help to answer some of the regular questions you receive. Whilst eBay offers this with the sale of an item, it's also straightforward to include an FAQ section in your own website.

Telephone: A contact telephone number is often the easiest way to answer enquiries, answer questions potential customers may have and, consequently, close a sale. However, it can be time-consuming and distracting, with many calls not resulting in a sale.

> ## Hot Tip
> Build up an FAQ section in your website by copying queries from emails you've received and posting the answers to them.

 Live chat: A message box can be incorporated into a website to enable potential customers to exchange messages with you and ask questions. It enables you to manage multiple queries at the same time (unlike a telephone call), allocate specific time to do this and assure customers you are genuine. Live chats are provided by specialists such as www.clickandchat.com, www.liveperson.com, www.whoson.com and www.websitealive.com, with prices ranging from monthly subscriptions of around £/$30 to one-off payments of a few hundred.

Above: With sophisticated seller ratings on sites such as eBay that can ruin your reputation, you need to make sure you respond promptly to any queries and communicate with your customers.

Ratings and Reputation

Dealing with customer enquiries can be the downfall of an online business. They can take up an excessive amount of time and lead to minimal sales, but if you don't deal with them they can ruin the reputation of a business. Customers may ask the most obvious questions, but if it helps to assure them that they can buy what they want, you need to see the point in answering their queries. By doing this, you can establish an honest and reliable reputation, which will be reflected through forums and any relevant ratings if you use eBay, Amazon and similar selling websites.

Managing Sales and Payments

Online sales require a fully organized system of ensuring orders are correct and money is received to avoid problems of misplaced orders and goods not received. The following pages outline what you need to do and who can help.

Sale Procedures

It's important to establish a system of recording and tracking sales to ensure every aspect can be checked. This may appear obvious, but if a customer doesn't receive an order and you can't find the details, or payment isn't received, then you need a fool-proof system to ensure such problems are quickly resolved. The following checklist will help to decide how you should manage sales:

- **Sale details**: Have you got all the necessary details concerning the sale, including what the customer is ordering, quantity and any special requirements? Such detail must be straightforward for the customer to complete online, even if you are using a third-party seller such as eBay or Amazon.

- **Customer information**: Make sure you can retrieve all essential customer information. This is not only required for delivering the goods, but also for identity checks and payment. In some cases, a billing address may be different to a delivery address.

Payment: Depending on the payment method used, can you check whether payment has been received? If you have several orders of the same value, can you identify which payment applies to which order?

Confirmation and updates: Customers expect to be informed about their order and many sellers now realize the value of this. An email should be sent to the customer to confirm an order, then another when the goods are dispatched. Some delivery companies provide text messages with delivery time slots and the option to rearrange to another time or date.

Honesty and ratings: It's important to establish an honest and reliable reputation, especially when using selling websites such as eBay and Amazon. Whether you are dealing with a few sales or several thousand, your future sales depend on what current customers think of your service.

Payment Procedures

There are many methods for receiving and making payments, most of which carry a cost and require some sort of organization. Whilst paying suppliers can be kept simple with invoices, receiving payments can become more complex, especially if you want to keep the cost of payments low (fees and commission) to maximize profits. The popular methods of payment are as follows:

Hot Tip

Many websites that sell items display a security certificate to help assure customers of their authenticity.

 PayPal: This has become an increasingly popular method of payment and whilst it's essential for a seller to hold a PayPal account, it isn't required for a buyer, who can pay with a credit or debit card. Fees are competitive with other payment methods and incur a standard charge of around £0.20 or $0.30, plus a percentage ranging from 1.4–3.4% of the sale price. A PayPal account can be viewed online and operated as a bank account, with the ability to use a credit balance to pay for fees and purchases.

 Google checkout: A similar service to PayPal, with a username and password required for the customer to make a payment using a credit or debit card that is already registered with his/her account. Payment fees for the seller are similar to PayPal. Thanks to Google's worldwide presence, this method of payment is becoming increasingly popular.

 Credit/debit card: Third-party payment collectors such as Worldpay can take payment online using a variety of credit and debit cards, providing a seamless method of payment on your website. These organizations look after the entire process of payment (including emails to the customer). Costs usually involve a monthly subscription, with fees of 1–2% on each transaction.

 Bank payment: Some online sellers offer discounted prices for using a bank payment, which incurs lower fees or no fees at all. In some cases, the customer has to contact the seller to be informed of the seller's bank sort code and account number, plus a reference. The customer then contacts his/her bank and arranges a payment to the seller. Whilst this method is often cheaper for all concerned, the customer has no means of protection from fraud (unlike card payments).

 Cheque/postal order: This is one of the slowest methods of payment, requiring a cheque or postal order to be posted to the seller, banked and cleared before the goods can be dispatched. The customer has no means of fraud protection (unlike card payments), but it's a cheap method for receiving payments and is useful where the customer has to deliver something, such as a rechargeable battery pack for refurbishment, or a picture for framing.

Payment Assurances

One of the hardest aspects of making a sale, whether it's over the internet or not, is ensuring money is exchanged. This potential problem is a worry for both buyer and seller. Some sales transactions can be stored in a holding fund until the goods are delivered. This helps to assure the buyer they have made a payment, but have a means of retrieving those funds if a dispute arises. It also assures the seller that payment has been made. Payment methods such as PayPal offer this service.

Delivery

The delivery of purchased items is not just essential to ensure a customer receives the goods they have bought, it's also one of the key aspects of building your business reputation. It ensures customers will return and any ratings on eBay, Amazon and other selling sites remain good. However, there are many potential pitfalls concerning delivery, which are covered over the following pages.

Delivery Planning

The cost of delivery can remove a large chunk of your profit if it is not correctly costed or built into the price of the goods. The following aspects need to be taken into consideration to avoid over- or underpricing delivery:

Above: This bubble-wrap machine can save a fortune on buying in large quantities of the finished product, but the cost of the machine must be accounted for in the delivery costs.

 Packaging: It may only seem like an envelope and label, but it's worth costing the price of these raw materials and the time taken to wrap an item. Also consider any equipment you may need, such as a bubble-wrap machine and a printer for address labels.

 Time to post: Whether your local post office is round the corner or a half-hour drive, the time and cost of taking an item to be delivered must be accounted for and included as a cost. Consequently, it may be cheaper to pay for a courier to collect items.

Delivery Deals

Many courier services and delivery companies offer discounted rates according to the volume of deliveries you provide for them. In many cases, the greater the number of deliveries, the larger the discount. However, this type of cost-cutting approach can have a detrimental effect, where cost-cutting leads to deliveries without a signature upon receipt or piecemeal-paid workers who are only concerned with making the delivery, even if it means leaving it in the back garden. Customers cannot appreciate a cheap delivery cost if it means their purchased goods do not arrive or arrive in poor condition.

Delivery Disasters

Most mail-order companies will use a number of delivery services. Whilst they may have struck a cheap deal with one particular organization, they will have a more expensive backup, just in case a problem arises. When the author ordered several books from a large internet-based seller, the books were delivered by a third-party courier, but placed in the recycling bin and the bin was emptied before they were retrieved. The second delivery was completed by another company, who were more expensive, but also more reliable and ensured the delivery was signed for.

> # Did You Know?
> **Items sold on eBay are rated by customers according to delivery costs. If you overcharge, your ratings may be affected.**

Selling Software

The logistics of selling items on the internet can become time-consuming with countless hours spent photographing products, creating listings and managing the process of selling, from stocktaking to dispatching orders. Fortunately, there is a wide range of programs and tools to help, some of which are available with particular online selling services.

eBay Selling Tools

Sales websites such as eBay have allowed people to turn a hobby into a profession and businesses to change from high-street to online selling. Consequently, managing the volume of sales, including creating listings, watching items for sale and assessing sales data, has turned into a whole new set of selling tools offered by eBay.

Fast Listing

eBay offers a program called Turbo Lister, which as its name suggests, provides a faster method of listing items. It's free to download and use, and promises to be quicker than completing the standard online form for a listing. The program can save listings for reusing in the future, provides easier editing of listings and has a wider range of screen controls (tool bar and menu options) enabling listings to be far more quickly produced.

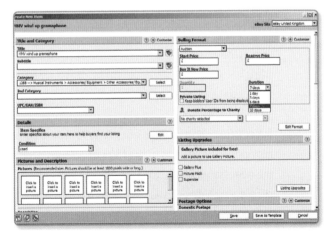

Above: eBay's Turbo Lister program is free to download and offers a faster method of adding listings.

Selling Manager

Selling Manager is an online tool aimed at medium-volume sellers to help manage and track their listings on eBay. It can help to monitor active listings, manage large amounts of feedback, and print out invoices and labels on a large scale. Selling Manager is part of your 'My eBay' and is free to use, plus it can be used in conjunction with Turbo Lister.

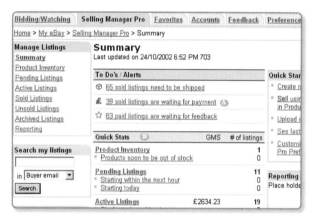

Above: eBay's Selling Manager Pro provides online management of listings, including alerts to low stock levels and notifications sent to buyers.

Selling Manager Pro

Whilst the aforementioned Selling Manager is free to use, Selling Manager Pro provides a wider range of tools and is either included in some eBay accounts or incurs a monthly subscription fee. It's suitable for eBay sellers who have a large volume of listings. This online selling tool helps to create listings, manages inventory, will automatically relist items, produces automatic notifications for buyers concerning orders, payments and dispatch, and will alert you to low stock levels.

Sales Reports

Successful selling through eBay requires some careful analysis of your past performance. eBay provides such analysis in the form of Sales Reports, which is free to use (providing you meet the necessary criteria), or Sales Report Plus, which provides a wider range of sales data. The differences between the two levels are as follows:

 Sales Reports: Providing you have an eBay seller's account in good order with a feedback score that exceeds 10, and have sold at least one item in the last four months, you can subscribe for free to receive Sales Reports. This entitles you to sales data including total sales, total fees and summary information on average sale price, ended listings and successful listings.

 Sales Reports Plus: In some cases this is free. In the UK, it's free to a seller with an eBay shop, but otherwise it costs £3 per month. It provides a wider range of sales analysis, including everything you get with the simpler Sales Reports. Data on fees is broken down, buyer statistics include a percentage of repeat buyers, sales are defined by category and types of listing are analysed to see which methods are the most effective.

DIY Selling Tools

It's easy to become entangled in the data surrounding sales, stock and buyer behaviour. So if you are left wondering how to analyze your sales performance, it may be best to begin with a do-it-yourself, common-sense approach. Simply list the items you have sold on a piece of paper or in a spreadsheet, along with relevant values for costings, sale price, delivery charges and fees to be able to see how much profit has been made. Include data such as time spent and you will quickly be able to build a picture of how your sales are performing.

> ## Hot Tip
> eBay's selling and analysis tools are useful for anyone with a medium or large volume of sales.

Simple Spreadsheet
A simple spreadsheet may be all that's required to help analyze online sales and costings. A spreadsheet program such as Microsoft Excel can filter data, create calculations (for example, percentage markup) and sort values to help make sense of large volumes of sales. For further information on this subject, see Flame Tree Publishing's book *Microsoft Excel Made Easy*.

Researching Sales Data

Another angle to sales data is to look at other people's sales information, especially sellers who offer the same products as you. This can be quickly compiled by searching through online selling websites for the products you sell to see what other sellers are offering, how much they charge and any finer points including delivery costs.

Social Network Sales Data

Potential online customers can be found not only through selling websites, but also through social network sites and similar community-based websites. Facebook and YouTube, for instance, offer voting buttons for subjects to allow members to like or dislike particular subjects or products. This could provide vital sales data or inform research into new markets.

Selling Trouble

What happens when a buyer complains about an item you have sold to them, doesn't pay or wants a refund? How do you deal with poor ratings that could affect future sales? When you go on holiday, who looks after your orders? Such dilemmas and more are discussed over the following pages.

Complaints

Online sellers including eBay and Amazon have strived to create an image of honesty. Where a buyer and seller behave appropriately by paying and delivering promptly, they are encouraged to reflect this in their respective ratings. This is essential for both parties to ensure other people can see that they are honest and will trust them in the future. However, as a seller, you need to be prepared for complaints.

Avoid Complaints

There are a number of precautions that can be taken to avoid complaints. These include the following:

Answer enquiries: Try to answer enquiries quickly and make sure the tone of the answer is helpful, even if the question is pointless or the answer is obvious.

☑ **Keep in contact**: Make sure a buyer is kept informed from the moment an order is made to when it is dispatched and delivered. Some of these tasks can be completed automatically.

☑ **Be honest**: Don't omit information that may lead to a complaint. For example, if you are selling a used guitar, make sure you clearly outline any damage using text and photographs with the description of it.

☑ **Clauses**: Include standard text that covers you for any typical complaints or problems that may arise. eBay provides the following standard text for second-hand goods: 'The item may have some signs of cosmetic wear, but is fully operational and functions as intended.'

☑ **Know the law**: Obtain advice and information on the law for your country that governs the sale of goods.

Complaints Policy

It's important to determine a complaints procedure, which can easily be promoted through your website and any other websites you use. This should include the following:

☑ **Time to complain**: Decide on a number of days after a buyer has received an item in which they can complain about it, especially if the item is used.

☑ **Promise to reply**: Decide upon a number of hours or days in which you intend to respond to a complaint to reassure potential buyers you will deal with a complaint quickly.

✓ **Raise and log**: Use a simple method of logging a complaint and linking it to any goods sold or other dealings you have with the person making the complaint. This makes it easier to document, especially if legal action is taken.

✓ **Use the law**: Find out what legislation is applicable and whether any government bodies (for example, Trading Standards) can help. Such organizations may have procedures for dealing with complaints, which can be included in your complaints policy.

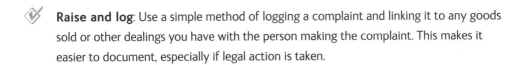

Non-payers

Payment methods such as PayPal and other credit and debit card transactions remove the risk of not receiving payment for an item sold, but what happens if someone wins an auction on eBay, but doesn't pay, or pays a deposit, but never pays the outstanding balance? In the case of eBay, this is where ratings can help and negative feedback can be left to clearly explain the case when a buyer does not pay. If a deposit is required, make sure you stipulate a maximum period of time before the buyer must pay the outstanding balance.

> ## Did You Know?
> eBay's Unpaid Item Assistant can help with purchases that are not paid for. *See pages 248–50 for more details.*

Returns

Expect a small percentage of goods to be returned for a variety of reasons. Consequently, it's worthwhile setting out a returns policy that clearly states whether items can be returned and, if so, how soon they need to be returned. There are many categories of goods, some of which should not be returned and others which need a number of clauses to avoid problems:

- **Material that can be copied**: CDs, DVDs and other media that can be copied should not be returnable unless they are defective, in which case a replacement must be dispatched if available.

- **Used goods**: Damage and defects must be clearly stated in the description. This will help avoid returns that state a reason that was already noted in the description.

- **New but cheap**: Many goods are considerably cheaper online than in high-street shops, but the price difference can sometimes be reflected in the quality. Explaining this point may dissuade some potential buyers, but it's often better to be honest.

Holidays

Making money on the internet requires you to regularly monitor your income and expenditure, and you need to be contactable to answer queries and deal with any problems that arise. It may feel like you can never leave your computer, but everyone needs a holiday or break at some point. If during this time you cannot find someone else to continue with your work, or you cannot be contacted, there are some solutions to avoid losing business:

- **Holiday notice**: Some online selling websites allow an 'On holiday' notice to be displayed alongside any goods you are selling. This allows potential buyers the opportunity to return and buy at a later date.

✅ **Auto email**: Many email services and programs have an out-of-office automated reply, which can be customized to explain you are on holiday and when you intend to return.

✅ **Receptionist service**: Some small businesses use a receptionist service, where their telephone number is diverted to another organization that handles the calls and passes on messages. This can be useful for holidays and times when you are not available. Prices vary, but most appear to be charged on a monthly basis.

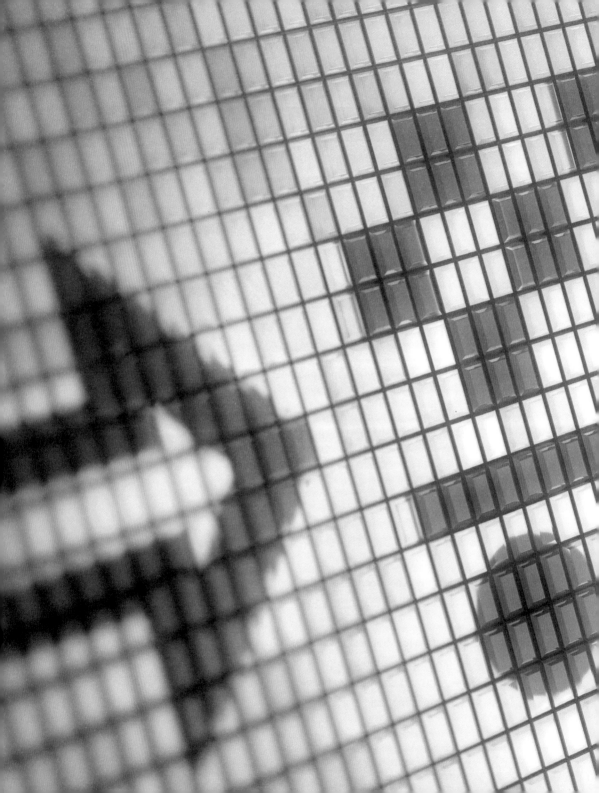

Make Money From Your Website

Become an Expert

Websites that offer advice on anything from DIY to investments can come to be regarded as not only informative, but also authoritative on their subject. Once this recognition has been earned, there is scope to generate income from it. The following section shows how to do this and where the money can come from.

Find Your Speciality

Spend a lot of time researching and thinking about what you would like to dedicate your expert status to. You may not be very knowledgeable at present, but as you progress, you will learn and gain sufficient experience and expertise to be of use and interest to others. Most people turn a hobby into such a profession, but you may want to think about whether the interest in that hobby will be lost.

Are There Other Experts?

Once you've decided upon your speciality, research other experts in the same field. Don't just look on the internet. Look for books that cover this subject, newspaper and magazine articles or columns and television programmes. Find out how they have gained expert status and whether they have a website similar to what you're planning to produce.

Right: Martin Lewis has become a recognized financial expert through his website, MoneySavingExpert.com.

What Do You Want?

Some expert or specialist websites are established as an extension of someone's hobby, offering them the chance to test products, receive all the latest news and get some discounts on related equipment. Some of these websites have turned into full-time jobs for their creators. It's important to determine how far you want to take a website and what you want to realistically achieve through it.

Hot Tip

Don't be afraid to turn into a minor celebrity through your website. People will want to know who you are, so include photographs and information on yourself.

Success Story – Expert Photographer

Professional photographer Joshua Dunlop runs the website www.expertphotography.com, which includes product reviews, tutorials, hints and tips and assessment of other people's photographs. The website allows Joshua to promote his photographic skills and win contracts for work ranging from portraiture and weddings to corporate and studio assignments. The website also generates direct income through Google Ads and other affiliated click-throughs such as PayPal. Elements to the website that are particularly successful include a blog, competitions and tutorials.

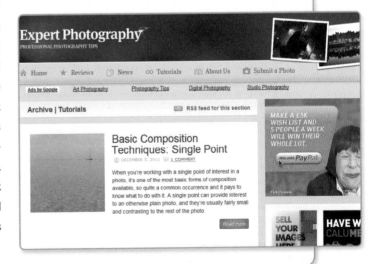

Plan to Promote

Your website is where you build your reputation. That requires an audience, so it's important to be able to draw people to your website. Promotion is covered in depth in chapter five (Make a Website), but here are a few points worth noting:

- **Selling websites**: If you sell something that is connected with your area of expertise and use an online selling website, you may be able to include a link to it from here.

- **YouTube**: Produce a video covering some of the topics you specialize in. This will help to generate publicity for you and a link to your website can be included. Online tutors often produce short taster videos explaining a specific subject, which helps to promote their website.

- **Forum discussions**: Get involved in forum discussions that are related to your subject of expertise. It may take time to gain recognition, but once that has been achieved, you can start to promote your website.

- **Social network groups**: Groups including Facebook and Twitter allow experts to express their opinions and offer advice, which can help to direct visitors to your website.

Above: Facebook is a very active social network that can be used to attract people interested in your hobby and to help develop your own website.

Establishing Interest

The reason for visiting a specialist or expert website is often to obtain information, whether it's technical advice or looking for the latest discounts and offers from specific businesses. Consequently, it's important to effectively plan your website and make sure its content is up to date and relevant to ensure visitors will return. Some suggestions for content include the following:

- **News**: Any news that relates to the subject you cover is essential. It helps to give the impression that the website is up to date and on the ball. Plus, it shows you have access to current information, re-enforcing your authoritative status.

- **Blog**: Regular comments from you about what you're doing. If, for example, your website covers the renovation of houses, a blog could show the current progress of a restoration.

- **Competition prizes**: Businesses connected with your subject may be willing to donate goods or services as competition prizes. This will not only help attract visitors, but establish a list of contact details and provide feedback to the supplier of the competition prize.

Blog

It's not a skin diseease, it's old underseal

By rhpress, Dec 13 2011 8:46AM

This is what I looked like after scraping off the old underseal from the underneath of my Bay. I started scraping off the old underseal in August 2010, taking roughly 3-4 hours per wheel arch to remove the old brittle black stuff, then applied a couple of coats of fresh underseal from an aerosol can. I've used products from Comma, Holts and Car Plan, which all sell for around £4-£6. The underfloor was a little more involved. I started scraping it off in 2010 and applied a couple of coats. Then in 2011 I took the van for an MoT and some welding repairs underneath were spotted by the MoT tester at MJ Motors (01924 472404), who advised they could be improved to avoid future corrosion. An inner sill and outrigger were duly repaired and the underseal applied again, but this time using an air fed spray gun, which provided a thicker covering. We also sprayed wax into the chassis rails and hidden cavities. I'll post more details on this on the restoration page and I've got a few rust proofing articles to cover for the VW mags and general motoring mags.

0 comments ✈Tweet ⓕLike

BLOG DIRECTORY

Welcome to my blog

This blog contains comment news on what I've done to Window Camper and the e and dreams I have for it - if cash. Please post comment that someone out there rea

Above: Adding a blog to a website helps to keep a website up to date and entice visitors to return. Chapter five (Make a Website) shows how to add a blog to your own website.

Hot Tip

Search the main news websites, including www.msn.com and www.reuters.com to find any relevant news that can be included in your website.

Discounts: Similar to competition prizes, businesses are often willing to offer a discount through a website to help monitor traffic and determine whether the website is useful for promotion. It is also a useful method of attracting repeat visitors.

Returning Interest

Tempting people to return to your website can only be achieved if they know something new will appear that is of benefit or interest to them. This may be new competitions or offers for discounts (outlined in the previous section), the latest news or an update to a blog. There are also several methods of communication, such as emailing messages or a monthly newsletter and joining a social network such as Twitter or Facebook.

Making Money

As your specialist website becomes established and popular, you have the opportunity to develop some sources of income from it. These include the following:

 Affiliate advertising: Relevant products and services can be advertised on your website, which can be bought by clicking through to the respective supplier. Some businesses offer affiliate advertising packages, which are covered in more depth later in this chapter.

 Sell products/services: If you can take orders for specific products or services, even if they are supplied by someone else, you can take a commission from the sale. This is similar to affiliate advertising, but allows you to handle the sale.

 Advertising: Businesses associated with the subject you cover may want to advertise on your website. This is a traditional method, which is still popular and simple to include. The number of people who click through to the advertiser's website can be measured.

Discounts/Free goods: Businesses may be willing to offer discounted or free goods or services in return for publicity through the website. For instance, if you're showing how to restore some antique furniture, a supplier may be willing to give you some tools or materials.

Success Story – Martin Lewis

Martin Lewis is a journalist who has become well known for providing independent money-saving information and tips on everything from cutting bills to finding the best offers for savings and credit cards. His website, www.moneysavingexpert.com, has become an essential money-saving resource for millions of people and Martin's fame has resulted in regular appearances as an expert on a wide range of television programmes. His success and exposure has led him to

becoming involved in various finance-related campaigns and charity work. Moneysavingexpert.com is regularly updated with the latest offers and discount vouchers, plus you can sign up to weekly emails, complete an online budget planner, visit a number of forums to get involved in discussions, and follow Martin on his blog, Twitter and Facebook. The website is free of advertising, but if the site is talking about a product and that discussion includes links, click-throughs on these may result in revenue for the site.

Turn a Hobby or skill Into Cash

Whether you're renovating your home or enjoy playing the piano, the internet can be a useful platform for publicizing what you're doing, attracting interest and potentially making some money. The following pages provide some thought-provoking ideas as to how you can achieve this.

Website Content

Your website needs to become a focal point for anyone interested in the subject you're covering. For instance, if you're interested in antique clocks, your website could include historical information, photographs, links to people who sell and repair clocks, and reviews of books. This can help to determine how and where you can earn money in the form of advertising and selling.

Keep Them Coming Back

If you want repeat visitors to your website, you need some way of attracting them back. This can include the following:

Left: Facebook allows members to add their interests, likes and dislikes, which can prove useful in finding people who will be the target market for a website that covers the subjects they are interested in. These people can be contacted via Facebook.

Forum: Incorporating a forum allows discussions to be conducted and draws people in (especially if they post a topic and are emailed when someone replies).

Blog: A blog provides the opportunity to keep in contact with people who visit the website and want to read your latest news.

Social network: Link through to social network sites such as Facebook and Twitter and you can draw people to your website and create a hobby-based community.

Webcam: If you're working on a project related to your hobby, or want people to see a location based around your hobby (a surfing website with live images of the sea showing the waves), incorporate a webcam to tempt people to return.

Success Story – Bird Watching to Bird Boxes

Lionel Haines has turned his ornithological hobby into an online business with the help of the internet. After developing a bird nesting box with an integrated webcam, he launched www.camnest.co.uk to help promote sales of his nesting boxes. Video footage and additional photographs of nesting birds are included in the website to help show customers what they get for 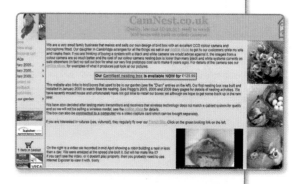 their money. Despite operating in Britain, Lionel now lives in France and lets other family members deal with the dispatching of goods and, in the future, the manufacturing too. Sales can be conducted securely online using credit or debit cards via Sage Pay.

Latest news: Search through the main news websites for any relevant news and post it. Speak with specialists and retailers connected to your hobby and make sure you are on their mailing lists.

Hot Tip

Find your competition first. If you have an idea for a website, see if it has already been done and whether you can do it better.

Third-party Links

A website's content isn't the only element that will attract visitors. Make sure you have links with similar websites and businesses. Consider uploading videos to YouTube and other video-hosting websites (see chapter six, Other Money-making Ideas) to link back to your own website. If you sell goods associated with your website, consider selling them through eBay and Amazon with links to your website.

Money Makers

The ways to make money through a hobby-related website are very similar to those outlined in the previous section of this chapter, which covers setting up a website and becoming an expert. The advantage with a hobby website, however, is that you can look at ways of funding your hobby or keeping costs low by reviewing or testing products and showing how to use products. Suppliers let you have the products for free in return for publicity.

Simple Success

Sometimes it's the simple and straightforward things in life that can lead to success. Take Hendrik Pohl's website and YouTube videos, which show how to tie a tie in a variety of ways. Some of his YouTube videos have each received between two and four million viewings! They provide clear instructions under simple titles, making them easy to follow and find.

Above: Hendrik Pohl's YouTube videos on how to tie a tie may sound simple, but some of them have received around four million viewings and helped to direct traffic to his website.

that contains tie-related instructions. All of these features help to boost the website's ratings with search engines such as Google and help to spread the word concerning Hendrik's website.

Tie-a-tie Money Makers

Tie-a-tie.net generates income using the following products:

Sale of ties: These can be bought online.

Video series: Hendrik has produced a series of videos, which can be bought and downloaded for $6.95.

Link to www.tie-a-tie.net

Hendrik's YouTube videos include a link to his website at www.tie-a-tie.net. Here there is more tie-related information, such as advice on dress codes for job interviews. There are also links to Facebook, an option to link to the website within your own website, and a contact page. Hendrik has also included a free web application that visitors can add to their Facebook profile or Google startpage

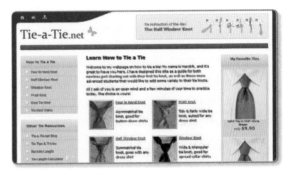

Above: The website www.tie-a-tie.net generates income from the sale of ties and instructional videos. This simple idea has generated lots of attention and was even broadcast by CNN in the USA.

Did You Know?

Hendrik Pohl's tie-a-tie.net website and YouTube videos may sound simple, but they caught the attention of US TV network CNN and were broadcast to millions of people.

Run a Review Website

Websites ranging from city guides and restaurant reviews to worldwide sites such as Trip Advisor and Campsite Review have become increasingly popular for people who want to know more about a place or business before they try it out and people who want to become online critics. Setting up such a website can be financially rewarding.

Find a Purpose

It's important to decide upon a purpose for a review website and what you would like to get from it. If, for instance, you want to produce a website that reviews restaurants local to you, this could be a great excuse to dine out. If, however, you want to generate some serious income from a website, you may want to concentrate on creating a website with wider appeal that can provide various methods of income.

Review Ideas

There are various types of review websites, which are often dependent on the subject being covered. Some of them are difficult to develop into an independent review site, and become information listings instead. The following list outlines the popular types:

Left: Websites www.freeindex.co.uk and .com offer free listings for businesses along with independent reviews. The websites generate income from discreetly placed advertising (such as Google Ads) and their premium subscription service.

Product reviews: These are suitable for including with the hobby-based or specialist websites covered earlier in this chapter. For instance, if you're running a website on landscape photography in your region, you could include product reviews of cameras and equipment available at a local shop.

 Service listings: Google and many websites provide listings for plumbers and other emergency and non-emergency tradesmen. Some of these websites include reviews.

 Leisure guides: Online tourist guides, restaurant reviews and hotel-booking websites are some of the subjects that can be covered.

 Interest guides: A hobby or interest can be turned into an informative website and include reviews or overviews of products and services.

Undercover Reviews

Restaurant, hotel and similar review websites do not generally rely upon expense-free exposure. Reviewers pose as normal customers and post their reviews afterwards. Consequently,

if you're planning to run such a website, consider whether you can afford to conduct this type of testing or whether you can find other people willing to pay their own expenses and post their own comments.

Success Story – City and Villa Guides

Paul Malish is the founder and owner of a number of successful UK-based online city guides (for example, www.leeds-city-guide.com) and a guide to privately owned rental properties and holiday villas in Florida, USA, focused on the Orlando area (www.orlando-villa-guide.com). These guides feature a wide range of city activities, from bars and shopping to restaurants, hotels and transport. All relevant businesses are listed, but if they want further promotion, advertising starts at £60 per year. Other revenue is generated from general advertisements, Google Adsense, affiliate programmes with relevant retailers, sponsored content, local business partnerships and commission from linked

Above: Paul Malish has successfully developed a number of city guide websites along with this guide to privately owned rental properties and holiday villas in Florida, USA focusing on the Orlando area (www.orlando-villa-guide.com).

online hotel booking services. As many of his websites are Google's number one ranked search result for many of their relevant search terms (for example, 'Restaurants in Leeds', 'Nightlife in Leeds'), they are uniquely positioned to maximize and capitalize upon the revenue streams mentioned above. For example, his Leeds city guide website receives over 60,000 unique visitors every month.

Reviews Without the Expense

Some reviews do not incur costs, such as product reviews. In many cases, the products will be given to you free of charge, especially if the cost of them is low, such as computer software and books. It's not so easy to review a hotel or restaurant in the same way, as an arranged free visit would negate the concept of an undisclosed test. In such cases, this would be classed as a promotional overview (advertorial).

Informational Reviews

A review website doesn't have to assess every business and service listed. Instead, it could simply provide information on local restaurants, hotels and other services to help attract visitors. The advantage with such an approach is that any relevant business can be approached for advertising.

Hot Tip

Interested in the latest gadgets? See websites including www.t3.com, www.pocket-linkt.com and www.stuff.tv.

Content Creation

Many review websites rely upon other people's reviews to help rapidly build their content. Websites such as Trip Advisor have expanded worldwide thanks to the many amateur travel critics who are keen to post their opinions. Where such content cannot be generated, such as the review of a product that has yet to be released, content from visitors to the website can still be generated using blog and forum-style comments. This helps to keep an audience interested and participative. The following types of content should be considered for use on a review-style website:

 Video: One of the most effective methods of reviewing a product or service is to produce a short video.

 Reviews from other sources: Whilst it may be feasible to produce your own reviews, it may also be possible and easier to acquire reviews from other websites. Permission should be sought of course, and costs may be incurred in some cases.

✓ **Sponsored overview**: This is known as advertorial and it often generates more income, but therefore it can't be considered an independent review.

✓ **Forums and blogs**: Including a forum or blog allows visitors to post comments and become involved in the website.

> # Hot Tip
> **Many review websites use Twitter to help create discussions and links.**

✓ **Like and Tweet**: Include buttons for visitors to tweet a comment to their friends or state they like a product using their Facebook account.

Above: Adding these Twitter and Facebook buttons to a review helps to connect visitors and create links and discussions relating to your website.

Money Makers

The popular methods of creating income from an expert website, outlined at the beginning of this chapter, also apply to a review website. However, there are more extensive methods of income generation, which are linked to the businesses and products under review. These can include the following commission-based ideas:

> ### Hot Tip
>
> If you produce a tourist-based website for a town or region, look into tourism funding and grants, which may be available to help set up the site.

☑ **Bookings**: If bookings for a table in a restaurant, food from a takeaway or a room in a hotel are taken via your website, an arrangement can be made to charge a commission.

☑ **Affiliate sales**: Click-throughs leading to sales can receive commission. This type of affiliate advertising is covered later in this chapter.

Success Story – Restaurant Guide

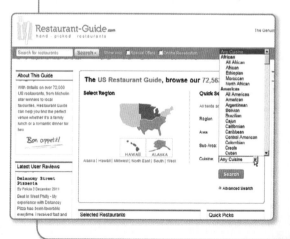

The website www.restaurant-guide.com (available in the UK, USA and EU) was started in Britain in 1997 by restaurateur and former President of the Master Chefs, Richard, 7th Earl Of Bradford. This review website has since grown extensively and now has over 15,000 listings in the UK, the same again across the EU and over 72,000 in the USA. It includes live bookings, which help generate further income for the website.

Make Money From Classifieds

A website can generate income from displaying advertisements, known as classifieds, posted by other people selling their goods. The following pages outline how to incorporate this method into a website and the various methods by which it can make money for you.

Classifieds

Classified listings that advertise other people's goods for sale is one of the traditional methods of selling, found on a number of websites. Whether it's a dedicated classifieds website, or an additional feature of an existing website, it's a useful way to make money. In most cases, an upfront fee is charged to place a classified advertisement for a specific amount of days.

Hot Tip

If you don't want the hassle of running classifieds on your website, include a link to a relevant classifieds website and see if you can arrange affiliate advertising from it.

DIY Classifieds

If you don't want to get involved in using software or a third party to host your classifieds, then the easiest approach is to do it yourself. This involves taking payment via a payment service such as PayPal and determining a means of receiving a seller's text (description) and photos to be able to add them to the classifieds section of your website. However, such an approach can be time consuming and it doesn't inspire the same degree of confidence in the seller.

Classifieds Software and Support

There is a wide range of paid-for and free classified services that can be used to provide classified advertisements on your website. There is often a catch with incorporating a free

Left: A basic e-Classifieds ad can be included in a website for free (as shown on the left of the picture), but you have to pay for more features – the sophisticated listing on this e-Vehicles page costs from $59.96 per month with a setup fee of $749.

classified service into your website, as it will probably be funded with advertisements or a commission will be charged for each classified advertisement. Free and paid-for classified software is available through Bravenet (www.braveapps.com/classified), www.e-classifieds.net, www.highlandclassifieds.com and many more (search for 'Add classifieds to your website').

Did You Know?

Classifieds can help to boost your website's ratings with search engines.

Success Story

VW Camper Crazy is an online classifieds website set up for selling second-hand VW campers. The website charges private individuals £10–£25 for placing an advertisement (price depends on the number of days the advertisement is displayed) and businesses can pay a fixed annual fee of £250 to post an unlimited number of advertisements. Other revenue is generated from advertisements for insurance companies and other sponsors, plus affiliate style click-throughs.

Affiliate Advertisements on Your Website

One of the main sources of income from websites is advertising. This has become more and more sophisticated in terms of finding new and original ways of promoting businesses and ensuring the advertising methods are effective. The following pages outline how to make money from a wide range of sources, from affiliate advertising to videos on YouTube.

What is Affiliate Advertising?

Also known as affiliate marketing, this is a sophisticated and evolved version of what was once known as a click-through. Using a range of advertisements and other methods of promotion on your website (such as a review of a business or product), visitors can click on links to associated businesses to make purchases, sign up for newsletters or register. This activity is traced back to your website and, depending on the affiliate agreement, you may receive a commission. There are various types of affiliate marketing, including the following:

Advertisements and offers: These are some of the most traditional methods of affiliate marketing, although they are now becoming more sophisticated and intuitive (*see* Cookie Tracing, page 142).

Left: Amazon's affiliate program provides commission for advertisements when visitors to your website click through and buy products from them.

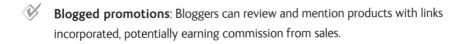 **Blogged promotions**: Bloggers can review and mention products with links incorporated, potentially earning commission from sales.

 **Social networks**: Similar to blogging, some social network sites allow affiliate links to be included.

Affiliate agents: Marketing specialists and websites such as Yahoo!, Amazon and Google act as agents for affiliate advertising, offering packages to include with your website. This is covered in greater detail later in this chapter.

> ### Hot Tip
> Look for links to affiliate advertising on commercial websites that sell goods online.

Commission on Purchases

Also known as pay per sale (PPS), this can be the most lucrative way of making money from your website. Some of the ways of directing sales and taking a cut include: displaying affiliate advertisements for people to click on; mentioning particular products in a blog; or reviewing products on your website.

Coupon Codes and Offers

Discounted sales and special offers are easier to trace back to your website, especially if a code has to be entered (known as a coupon code). The code can be spread through various forums, blogs and emails, allowing the seller to calculate total sales and pay you a commission.

Surveys and Sign-ups

If visitors to your website complete online surveys, register with a third party or sign up to their newsletter, a referral fee can be paid. In most cases, this is not as lucrative as sales commission, but it's an additional means of income.

Did you know?

Ever wondered how ads pop up in websites with products you've been looking at elsewhere? It's down to cookies storing this information.

Cookie Tracing

Affiliate advertising usually relies upon cookies to trace a lead or sale back to your website. However, these cookies often last for only 30 days before the trace expires. So if a customer clicks though from your website, but does not make a purchase until after the 30 days are up, you won't get paid a commission – unless the customer returns to your website and follows the link again.

Include AdSense in Your Website

Google AdSense

Welcome to AdSense   What is AdSense? | Do you already have an account?
Please complete the application form below.

Website Information

Website URL: www.robhawkins.co.uk
• Please list your primary URL only.
• Example: www.example.com

Website language: English — English
• Tell us your website's primary language to help our review process.
☐ I will not place ads on sites that include incentives to click on ads.
☑ I will not place ads on sites that include pornographic content.

Contact Information

Account type: Individual
Country or territory: Select an account type:

! Important - Your payment ... below. Please complete all fields that apply to your address, such as ... name and house or apartment number and accurate country, Postcode and city. Example.

Payee name (full name):
• Your Payee name needs to match the name on your bank account.
• Payee must be at least 18 years of age to participate in

Above: Google AdSense is straightforward to join. The HTML code used to feature these money-making advertisements needs to be copied into your website.

Google AdSense offers a variety of ways of including affiliate advertising in your website, blog or forum. These methods include relevant advertisements on the contents page of your website, a search box for visitors to use, and links to advertisers that relate to your website. In all cases, revenue is generated by clicking through to the advertisers' websites. The fees paid by the advertisers vary, but the commission you receive is fixed at 68% in the case of AdSense for Content (an advertisement on your website's contents page) and 51% for search results.

Did You Know?

Google AdSense and other similar affiliate programs can be added to your website using website design software.

Sign Up to Google AdSense

Visit the Google website for your country and search for 'Sign up to Google AdSense' (or go to www.google.com/adsense). Navigate your way to a sign-up screen. Here you will need to enter details concerning your website address, where you are based, how Google can contact you, and what type of advertisements you don't want featuring (for example, pornographic).

Incorporate Google AdSense Into Your Website

Copying and pasting the HTML code required to run an advertisement (content) or search box is the preferred method for including AdSense in your website. Simply copy it after signing up, then paste it into the relevant web page using an HTML editor or website design software.

Hot Tip

See www.adbrite.com and www.bidvertiser.com for more ideas on making money from advertising.

Success Story – FreeIndex uses Google Ads

Website www.freeindex.co.uk has used Google Ads since 2006, including the contents advertisements and search facilities. These are included on the Category and Profile pages of the website and were added by copy-pasting suggested HTML from Google. Over 3,000 categories of advertisements ranging from Dove Release to Driving Instructors appear on FreeIndex using Google Ads. The advertisements change according to whatever the visitor to the website is looking for.

Above: www.freeindex.co.uk uses Google Ads in the form of content advertisements and search results. The picture here shows Google Ads displayed in the bottom of the screen as automatic search results.

Success Story of a City Cottage

Teachers and writers Paul and Diana Peacock have successfully transformed their interest in cookery and self-sufficiency into an occupation via www.citycottage.co.uk with a cookery school, courses, books and nationwide media appearances. Their aim is to promote the concept of self-sufficiency for the inner city.

Above: Self-sufficiency and cookery website City Cottage is operated by husband and wife team Paul and Diana Peacock from their home in the North West of England.

Behind the Scenes

Based in Lancashire in the North West of England, Paul and Diana Peacock's City Cottage operates from the couple's home where they write their books, produce videos and hold cookery courses (other venues are also used at times).

Publicity Streams

Whilst Paul and Diana's main publicity centres around their website, they also use a wide variety of other resources to help generate publicity and draw in audiences. These include the following:

 YouTube: Cookery videos showing how to make food, work on your garden and look after animals such as chickens are hosted on YouTube. Just search for 'City Cottage' on YouTube and you'll find the Peacocks' channel.

Above: City Cottage's YouTube channel has helped to draw audiences from YouTube to Paul and Diana's website.

 Facebook and Twitter: Regular updates and discussions via these social network websites help to keep Paul and Diana looking active and in the limelight. Facebook is also a useful platform for publicizing the couple's overview of their City Cottage website.

 Online magazines: Paul and Diana have started to develop an online magazine relating to their specialist subjects. The first one is called *Good Life Living* and can be found at www.gltv.org.uk. It covers a variety of news relating to self-sufficiency and the food industry.

Content Winners

There are a number of categories of content within a website that help to raise its profile and make sure it appears high on the list of results with search engines. Paul and Diana have a news page, which can help to provide up-to-date information that search engines recognize.

They have also included a Google search box on this page. Their home page features a calendar, organized by Eventbrite, showing forthcoming cookery courses, and links to Facebook and Twitter. There's also a section to enable visitors to sign up for a newsletter and news that helps to show the website is current.

 Above: City Cottage generates income from the sale of cookery courses and books written by Paul and Diana Peacock. It has also helped to raise the couple's profile and Paul now appears on Radio Four.

Making Money

The main sources of income that Paul and Diana generate from their City Cottage website include the following:

✔ **Cookery courses**: A number of cookery courses are scheduled on City Cottage's website. Bookings for these courses are handled by Eventbrite, which also includes links to calendars within Outlook, Google, Yahoo! and iCal.

✔ **Books**: Paul and Diana have written over 25 books on the subject of cookery. These are available via their website and other book-selling websites including Amazon (paper and hardback, plus three e-book titles).

✔ **Appearances**: Paul is a panellist on Radio Four's 'Gardener's Question Time' and the couple are available for talks and seminars on cookery and self-sufficiency.

Success Story of the Frugal Chef

Mary Ann Allen is known as the Frugal Chef through YouTube and her own website www.thefrugalchef.com. The following section outlines how she uses a variety of resources ranging from Kindle to Facebook to publicize her cooking skills and earn a living.

Video

With nearly 500 videos uploaded to YouTube, Mary Ann Allen has her own channel called The Frugal Chef (look for her YouTube ID – pastryparrot1), which has over 11,000 subscribers and has received almost four million viewings since 2008! This YouTube channel has been customized with food-related graphics and provides a professional front to Mary Ann's business. Some

Above: Mary Ann Allen's YouTube channel (pastryparrot1) has over 11,000 subscribers and has received nearly four million viewings!

videos feature an advertisement that runs at first, but can be skipped after a few seconds. Her website (www.thefrugalchef.com) is displayed along the bottom of the video screen when a video is being played. Some videos include additional advertising along the bottom edge, which can be clicked on.

Video Marketing

Mary Ann has produced some personal and informative videos that cover a wide range of cookery and housekeeping subjects. Whilst the videos can only generate a small amount of income from advertising, the main aim of them is to direct visitors to her own website.

TheFrugalChef.com

Mary Ann's website is organized and easy to understand with clear headings along the top to help visitors find interesting information relating to cookery. There are a number of features that help to keep this website looking up to date, which is always favoured by search engines. These include the following:

- **Current date**: The present date is displayed in the top-left corner of each screen.

- **Social network links**: A 'Stay Connected' option near the top of each screen provides links through to social network sites including Facebook and Twitter and Mary Ann's YouTube channel. There are also additional links on the home page to Facebook.

- **Search box**: In the top-right corner of each page, there is a search box visitors can use to look for specific topics within the website.

- **Monthly newsletter signup**: This clearly indicates that the website has something new to offer every month.

- **Weekly savings**: Mary lists a wide range of grocery stores with links to their weekly savings coupons.

- **Posts and comments**: Visitors to the website can post comments regarding recipes and other subjects. This helps to show people are visiting the website and interacting with it.

Money Makers

The website uses a variety of methods to help generate income. These include the following:

- **Amazon e-books**: A link near the top of the screen goes direct to Amazon and Mary Ann's latest e-book, which can be purchased and downloaded.

Other e-books: A dedicated page within the website lists all of Mary Ann's e-books, with the option to purchase them using e-commerce software.

Country-specific Google Ads:
Rolling advertisements are displayed throughout the website, which are specific to the visitor's country. Even though Mary Ann lives in the USA, UK visitors see UK-related advertisements.

Rollover ads: Some advertisements only require the mouse to be positioned over them for music to start playing and the advertisement to pop out after a few seconds. These advertisements are displayed with a short animation clip to help attract attention.

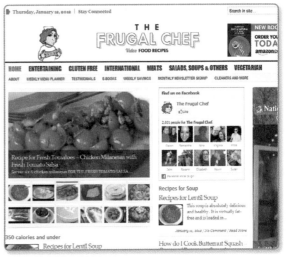

Above: Advertisements are often country specific on The Frugal Chef.

YouTube videos: A number of YouTube videos are used throughout Mary Ann's website to provide instructions on recipes, updates and money-saving tips. Many of these videos are run with advertisements.

Useful Design Tools

The Frugal Chef website is designed using WordPress software, which is free to use and very helpful for creating anything from a blog to a complete website. It also helps to incorporate some useful tools for visitors to the website. For example, there is a toolbar that can be displayed along the bottom of each page, which can be maximized or minimized. This toolbar includes a search box, a translation option, a link to YouTube, links to social network websites, and the option to begin a video chat.

Make a Website

Designing a Website

The starting point for creating a website is the design stage. At this point it's important to know what you want from your website and how you want it to look. Designing a website doesn't necessarily require the use of a computer, but it does require careful research and planning. The following section explains how this should be done.

Above: The aim of a website is one of its key aspects. Make sure visitors can find the content required to make a sale, click on advertising or somehow make money for you.

What's the Point?

The one question that you should keep in mind when designing a website is 'What is the point of it?' It's essential to keep thinking about the purpose of a website, especially when you discover more and more features to add to it and start generating an ever-growing number of ideas. Designers often talk about needs analysis – thinking about what you want from a design. Your answers should include the following:

 Make money: This could be the primary objective, but the website needs more elements to ensure people visit it and in turn make money for you.

 Attract particular visitors: An audience is essential, especially an audience with a specific interest that can make money for you.

Market Research

One of the most effective ways to design a website is to look at what your competitors are offering and see if you can do better. Don't just stick to websites in your own country; search worldwide through the various search engines from Google and Yahoo! Also, look at other industries that work in the same way as the website you plan to create. For instance, if you plan to create a website covering the renovation of a house, look at websites that cover the restoration of cars.

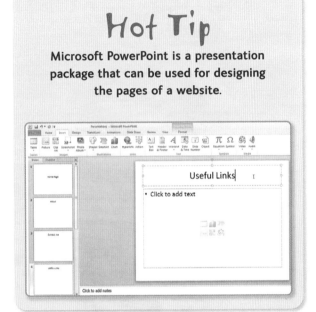

Hot Tip

Microsoft PowerPoint is a presentation package that can be used for designing the pages of a website.

Design on Paper

Websites with multiple pages are often easier to design on pieces of paper. This method allows you to make a list of subjects and aspects you want to cover, then write them into the relevant pieces of paper that represent the different pages of the website. Most designers use a hierarchical structure for designing web pages, with an introduction or home page at the top, then sub-pages below and, if necessary, more pages below these.

Design Colours and Themes

Look at lots of colour schemes on different websites to help you decide which ones work and which ones look unsuitable. Experiment with different colours, fonts and styles using word-processing or DTP software. This will help to settle upon a particular set of colours, fonts and other styles that can be applied throughout your website.

Hot Tip

Avoid using too many colours and fonts in a website.

Build Your Own Website

A website can be created in a number of ways, ranging from writing your own HTML code using a simple text editor to using an online creation package with web space and a domain name provided. The following section explains what options are available and how a website should be constructed.

Website Checklist

A website needs the following checklist of considerations:

- ☑ **Domain name**: A suitable website address.

- ☑ **Webspace**: A website-hosting service or a server to store the website's files.

- ☑ **Software**: A program of some description is required to construct the website, whether it's online or on your computer.

- ☑ **Email**: A message-forwarding service can provide multiple email addresses that contain your website address (for example, sales@robhawkins.co.uk), which are redirected to a specific email account.

> **Hot Tip**
> Your internet service provider at home may provide some online space, which can be used to host a website.

Build Options

The popular approaches to building a website are as follows:

- ☑ **HTML editor**: If you are familiar with writing in hypertext markup language (HTML for short), you can produce exactly what you need using something as simple as a text editor, such as Microsoft Notepad.

Web design software: Serif's WebPlus, Adobe's Dreamweaver and Microsoft's Frontpage are some of the web design programs that can help create an entire website. Some software is free to use, such as WordPress, whereas others are offered as trial versions with full versions ranging from a few pounds or dollars to a few hundred.

Above: The online Sitebuilder at www.domaincheck.co.uk allows the quick creation of a website, which can include a blog and photo gallery.

 Other programs: Word processors including Microsoft Word can export a file as a web page, allowing it to be used in a website. This is an easier approach to creating a website, especially if you are familiar with such a program, but the results may not be as good as using a dedicated program.

 Online design: There are lots of deals offering the online creation of a website, often for free (although advertising is usually included). If you are new to web design software, then a free online website may help to make you more familiar with what's required.

Online Website Design

The following step-by-step guide outlines what's involved in making your own website with an online web design program provided by www.moonfruit.com.

 Visit www.moonfruit.com: Open your web browser and go to Moonfruit's home page, where you will see a number of website designs on the screen. First, log in or register by clicking on the 'Login' button near the top-right corner of the screen. You will need to decide upon a username and password and enter details including your email address. After registering, you can choose to create a website – click on 'Add site'.

Above: Website www.moonfruit.com offers a wide range of styles for creating your very own website online.

Above: Enter a name for your website and an address, which will be followed by .moonfruit.com.

Pick a design: On Moonfruit's home page, you'll see a variety of website designs. Click on the arrows to flick through the different ones and when you find one you like, select it. The design will pop up in the centre of the screen. Select 'Click to build' to proceed.

Name and address: After selecting a website design, you'll need to enter a name for the site and an address. The site address will include '.moonfruit.com' at the end. So if you use an address such as 'FrenchGite', the full address will be www.frenchgite.moonfruit.com. After entering the site name and address, click on 'Launch my site' (if the address is already used, you'll have to enter another one).

Keep for free: Your Moonfruit site is only available as a free trial for 15 days, but can be converted to either a paid-for website with more features, or a free website with Moonfruit's own advertising and limited features (sufficient to get you started). A message box will prompt you and guide you through choosing a paid package or converting to free (the site has to be updated every six months to remain free).

✍ **Add content**: The online sitebuilder screen will display the web page design you chose. It can be edited by double-clicking inside text and changing it. Images and text boxes can be removed by selecting them and pressing delete on the keyboard. Other pages for your website can be opened and edited by selecting the appropriate navigation buttons.

✍ **Insert your own images**: Click on the Insert button near the top of the screen and a list of objects to insert will appear down the left side of the screen. Click on 'Image' on the left side of the screen and a File Manager window will appear. Select the images folder on the left, then click on 'Upload' to locate and add your own images from your computer. After uploading an image, select it and click on the 'Use this' button. You can then close the File Manager and move and resize your image on the web page.

Above: Images can be inserted into your website by clicking on 'Insert' near the top of the screen, then selecting 'Image' from the panel on the left. Your own images can be uploaded as shown here.

Above: Your website is immediately available to view online via Sitebuilder or by visiting your website address ending with .moonfruit.com.

✍ **Check and publish**: Your website can be instantly viewed online and is also available for anyone else to look at. Either click on the relevant button on screen, or use your web browser to visit your website address (the one ending '.moonfruit.com'). Your website can be further modified by logging into your account. Other features can be added including links to Facebook and Twitter.

Domain Names and Hosting

An easy-to-remember and relevant website address (domain name) is essential, but relatively easy to find and acquire. Domain name search sites including www.nameboy.com, www.123-reg.com, www.checkdomain.com and www.whois.net can check whether a domain name is already owned. If it isn't, you can shop around for a deal to purchase the name along with any web hosting packages and online web design services (if required).

> ## Hot Tip
> Many free website domain names are available, which include the provider's business name in the address or feature advertising with your website.

All-in-one Offers

If you haven't got a domain name and web space to host a website and are unfamiliar with HTML or web design software, it may be cost effective to opt for a package that includes all of these features with an annual or monthly payment. Web hosting services can provide all of this and there are plenty of them to be found through search engines such as Google and Yahoo! However, it's worthwhile speaking with them and making sure you're confident they are providing the correct advice and guidance. Look for web hosting services that are in your country and possibly local to you.

Left: Website www.domaincheck.co.uk provides a wide range of web-hosting packages, ranging from the basic to e-commerce sites. Using such a specialist can help with the technicalities of running a website.

Adding Content

There's a vast assortment of content available that can be added to a website, some of which is free to use. The following section outlines what you need to consider in the way of content and where you can access free material that helps to make your website look professional.

The Essentials

There are a number of categories of information that need to be included in your website to help avoid legal disputes and reassure customers you are genuine. These include the following:

- **About you**: It always helps to include a short section outlining who you are and what you do. If possible, include a personal angle, such as a photograph of yourself.

- **Legal paragraphs**: Include any relevant information on copyright of your website's content and legal disclaimers concerning the purchase of products and delivery. Look at other people's websites to see what is required.

- **Purchase protection**: Display the methods of payment you accept and if there are any security measures, promote this to reassure customers the website is genuine (for example, SSL or Verified by Visa).

Above: Essential information including contact details, terms and conditions and an 'About us' page are required to provide useful information to visitors to your website.

Contact details: A website needs to offer some method of communication to help deal with enquiries, purchases and complaints.

Avoiding Scams and Spam

One of the biggest threats for a commercial website is receiving an endless stream of spam emails and telephone calls from companies offering products and services you don't want. Many websites try to avoid this using the following methods:

Above: Adding a security question to a form helps to reduce the risk of spam.

 Contact details: Don't display your contact details as text because the information can be copied and used for sales calls. Instead, create an image for the contact details and add this to your website.

 Online forms: If you have any online forms for customers to submit questions, include a validation field where the submitter has to type in some words that are displayed as an image. This is difficult for automated programs to read and helps to avoid scams.

 Register first: Restrict access to your website unless visitors register and log in. Whilst this may deter some customers, it helps provide a level of security, which may reassure customers who want to make online purchases.

Keep It Clear

Make sure your content is clear and easy to understand. Avoid over-filling pages to make them difficult to read. Many websites are cluttered with affiliate advertising, search boxes and additional images, leaving very little space for the main content.

Copyright-free Material

Illustrations, photographs, artwork, video and animation are some of the elements that help to bring a website to life, but where do you find such material and do you have to pay a fee? There are lots of ways to obtain free material, including the following:

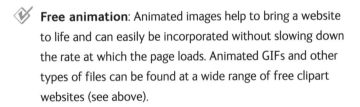

Above: Free clipart online can usually be copied by right clicking using a PC (Ctrl and click with a Mac). The copied image can then be pasted into an image-editing program and saved.

 Free clipart on your computer: Programs such as Microsoft Office and dedicated drawing programs such as CorelDraw include free-to-use clipart, which can be included in a website.

Above: Free animated images are available from a number of websites. These can be found at www.free-animations.co.uk.

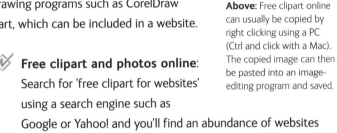 **Free clipart and photos online**: Search for 'free clipart for websites' using a search engine such as Google or Yahoo! and you'll find an abundance of websites offering free images.

 Free animation: Animated images help to bring a website to life and can easily be incorporated without slowing down the rate at which the page loads. Animated GIFs and other types of files can be found at a wide range of free clipart websites (see above).

 Other free stuff: Banners, sidebars, lines and buttons can all be found on free clipart websites.

Online website builders: If you use an online service to construct your website, this will probably include images and other features that can be included in your website for free.

Hot Tip

Don't copy images from other people's websites without their permission. It could result in a very expensive legal claim.

Including Video

One of the most effective elements of a website has got to be video. It allows you to get your message across in a professional manner, whether it's selling a number of products, offering a service or trying to assure potential customers they are dealing with a genuine organization. The following pages outline how video can be included and what the cost implications are.

Produce Your Own

You don't need expensive filming equipment and sophisticated audio devices to be able to record video for a website. Something as simple as a digital camera with low-quality video recording is sufficient. The key to successful video work is based on other elements including the following:

☑ **Good lighting**: Make sure you record the video in daylight or under good artificial lighting. The poorer the light quality, the grainier the video will look (unlike taking a photograph, where the flash will compensate for dull lighting).

☑ **Be quiet**: If possible, keep unwanted noise to a minimum so that anyone who needs to speak or make a noise in the video can be heard. Microphones on the simplest digital cameras are very good at picking up unwanted background noise.

☑ **Write a script**: Don't have the script in your head. Write it out and practise it several times.

☑ **Make a storyboard**: It may help to draw a series of pictures (storyboard) outlining the video, especially if you intend to piece together a number of clips.

Free Video Editing

Software including Windows Movie Maker is free to use and can be used to quickly edit a video, stitch several clips together, add effects and it will save it in a format that's suitable for uploading to a website or a video hosting site such as YouTube.

Use a tripod to help steady your camera or video camera.

Hosting Video

There are a number of methods for including video in a website. The popular approaches include the following:

Above: Uploading videos to YouTube is fast and straightforward. All you need is a free account and an internet connection.

 YouTube: Joining YouTube and uploading video to an account allows you to include video in your website. The only disadvantage is the video screen displays YouTube inside it. However, this is regarded as one of the cheapest and easiest methods of including video in a website, providing you know how to link it to your website.

 Host it yourself: If you have sufficient webspace and your provider allows video to be streamed, then video files can be uploaded and run with any suitable players. Web design software including DreamWeaver offers plug-ins to run video.

 Online web design: Some online web design packages include the option to incorporate video. This is rarely found with free website hosting, but can be included with subscription services.

Online uploads: Specialists such as www.easywebvideo.com provide an online video creation service, which allows you to upload a video and add features including an email link, PayPal button and logo.

Adding a Forum to a Website

A forum allows discussions to be held through your website, which is useful for a wide range of purposes, from gathering opinions on your products to providing online help. The following pages provide an outline of how a forum is included in a website and what potential problems can arise with it.

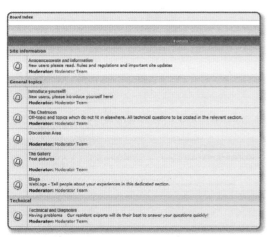

Above: Forums can cover a wide range of standard and customized topics.

Did You Know?

A forum is also known as a message board or bulletin board.

Why a Forum?

A forum provides a discussion platform, allowing you to communicate with a number of visitors, whether it's providing advice on your products or the service you offer, testing people's reactions with ideas you have, or just letting people discuss subjects and create traffic to your website.

Forum Advantages

There are numerous pros and cons to including a forum in your website. From a business point of view, a forum offers the following advantages:

 New products: You can promote products by opening discussions and obtain some market research based on people's opinions.

 Resolve problems: Typical problems concerning your website and the products or services it offers can be posted by people and you can see how many other people have had similar trouble. Plus, you can then offer solutions, creating a frequently asked questions (FAQ) page.

 Create a customer base: The details concerning numerous customers and potential customers can be generated and used for emails and other forms of communication.

 Links and advertising: A forum can include links to other areas of your website, to social network websites and affiliate advertising. This enables visitors to become more involved and hopefully spread the word about your website and what you are offering.

Forum Disasters

Running a forum within a website from which you are trying to make money can pose plenty of disadvantages, including the following:

 Sabotage: Competitors, scams and other trouble makers may try to join the forum and post anything ranging from negative opinions on you to offers for ink cartridges. A forum needs to be regularly monitored (policed) and inappropriate topics immediately removed.

 Time consuming: The amount of time spent responding to discussion topics can be considerable and many discussions never fully come to an end. You can easily spend several hours each day posting comments.

Defending yourself: Forum comments can be hurtful and negative, and it's sometimes difficult to defend yourself without digging an even deeper hole. Developing a thick skin is essential.

Argumentative members: Patronizing and belittling replies to questions and comments will only reduce the volume of visitors to a forum and, consequently, its effectiveness. Encourage people to make postings, but have a strict policy against offensive comments.

Hosting a Forum

There are two main types of forum that can be included in a website:

 Forum program: This is in the form of a script that creates and runs the forum. Popular scripts include PHP, CGI, Perl and ASP. If your website host allows such scripts to be run and you know how to include this in a website, then the forum can be operated from within your website. Some web hosting services and online design packages can include a forum.

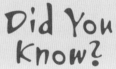

Did You Know?

An image linked to a forum member is known as an avatar. In most cases they need to be 120x90 pixels.

 Third party forum: An independent organization can run your forum, which is linked to your website, but often run as a separate part of it. In many cases, the forum cannot be embedded into your website.

Create a Free Forum

The following step-by-step guide outlines what is generally involved in setting up and operating a free forum:

 Find a free forum: There are lots of forums that can be set up and run for free. Use a search engine such as Google or Yahoo! to find a free forum, then look through several of them to find out if there any hidden costs or limitations.

Register: Once you have found a free forum you would like to create, the first step is to register with it and establish a name for the forum. Other details, including a contact email address and password to administer the forum, are usually required.

Confirmation: After setting up your forum, you'll receive an email confirming any relevant details. There may also be a link to click on to activate the forum. This email needs to be safely saved on your computer or within your email account.

Log in: Make sure you can log in to your forum as an administrator. This will enable you to change a number of details, such as a welcome message, rules for membership and postings and the categories for discussion.

Add profiles: If you want visitors to your forum to register and display some details concerning themselves, this is usually achieved by adding profile fields. These fields can be controlled by Yes/No tick boxes and numbers for dates.

Create new categories: Your forum will probably need a number of categories to help organize topics and posts. These can usually be set by adding them online once you are logged in as the administrator.

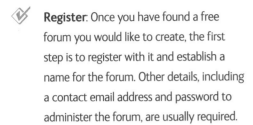
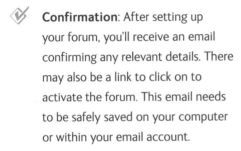

Above: Registering a forum involves providing details including a description, your email address and password to allow you to administer the site.

Above: After registering a forum, you will usually receive a confirmation email containing summary information to access and administer it.

☑ **Administer the forum**: It's important to regularly log in to your forum and monitor the progress of postings to help avoid malicious content and ensure members who have posted questions receive replies. A forum needs to remain active and current.

Making Money From a Forum

There are a number of ways to make money from a forum, including the following:

☑ **Advertising**: Depending on the type of forum you are operating and the organization that hosts it, you may be able to run advertisements through it, including affiliate advertisements.

☑ **Other links**: If you run an eBay shop or sell items using another method online, you can use the forum to create a link to any relevant websites.

☑ **Specialist publicity**: A forum can help you become established as a specialist or expert in a particular field, which may help with products that you sell and other websites you operate.

☑ **Additional asset**: A forum should be regarded as an addition to making money on the internet, allowing potential customers to be drawn in through this discussion platform.

☑ **Consultancy services**: If you are a specialist in a particular field, a forum is a useful marketing tool and platform on which queries can be answered and your services advertised.

Hot Tip

It's very easy for discussions to turn into arguments on forums, but this is bad for business and will inevitably lead to fewer visitors. Try to encourage discussions, but discourage offensive conflict.

Create a Blog

A blog has become one of the most effective internet marketing tools, allowing someone to post comments as a diary or journal and in turn generate an audience. Money can be earned from advertising, click-throughs, selling goods and services, and linking to other businesses.

Success Story of a Dutch Guitar Tutor

Guitar tutor Eddie de Hamer has his own website at www.guitartutorleeds.com and has included a blog, which he regularly updates with information, images and video links concerning different aspects of guitar playing. He has found that more people visit his blog pages than any other part of his website, and so he is currently expanding this side of the website to include links to videos stored on YouTube. Eddie's only means of making money from his website is to attract interest in guitar tuition and book courses with him. His website and the blog in particular appear to have led to more enquiries and subsequent bookings.

Right: Guitar tutor Eddie de Hamer has found the blog on his website has become the most-visited part of his website and helps lead to enquiries and bookings.

Blog Content and Types

There are various different types of blog according to their content and purpose. Whilst the traditional blog was originally set up to display comments in the form of text, many blogs can include photos, illustrations, links and video. Consequently, a whole new set of names has evolved including a vlog for video, linklog for links, sketchblog for sketches and a photoblog for photographs. A blog that contains a mixture of these is known as a tumblelog.

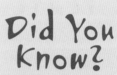

Blog Money Makers

There is a seemingly endless list of ideas for running a blog, but how many of these can make you money on the internet? Those that can include the following:

Above: Great British Sports Cars uses a blog to display their latest news and recent activities.

 Project work: If you're renovating your house, restoring a car, or reviving an old sofa, a blog can keep people interested and enable you to ask for discounts from specialists, for example, or run a related website with affiliate advertising.

 Reviews: Take any hobby ranging from gardening to literature and you can run a blog that provides reviews on the latest books or gardening equipment.

 Become an expert: Turn a hobby or interest into a blog and you can soon become recognized as an expert, where you can offer advice through your blog and attract sponsors and advertising.

 Sell your services: Whether you're a private tutor or a plumber, a blog is a useful platform to promote yourself and help sell your goods or services.

Behind the Scenes of a Blog

A blog can be as simple as a web page with comments listed in date order. This is very easy to set up and run (see earlier in this chapter for instructions on creating a web page), but isn't quite so easy to allow visitors to automatically post comments. Consequently, many bloggers prefer to use dedicated software or blog services that can be run and edited online or via your own computer.

Web Page or Forum

Setting up a web page to act as a blog is reasonably straightforward, requiring you to update the page every time you want to post a comment. This is relatively easy with many online web design services. However, it's also feasible to run a forum as a blog, enabling other people to post comments.

WordPress

This free software is available to download from www.wordpress.org and can be installed on a web server or home computer. It allows a blog to be fully managed and customized and the software has become one of the most popular methods of creating a blog or even a website.

Movable Type

This long-standing blog and website creation software first appeared in 2001 and has been continually developed. It's available to download for free from www.movabletype.com,

Above: Blog software such as Movable Type is free to download, although there are other packages available that can be bought.

although, there are other packages that can be bought. If you want a straightforward method of running a blog, Movable Type's free version is a popular choice.

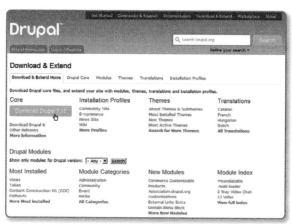

Above: Drupal is a popular open source software, which is free to download from www.drupal.org.

Drupal

Known as a Content Management System (CMS), this free-to-use software is a social networking application, forum and blogging tool, forming a framework for building all kinds of powerful web applications. Further details and free downloads can be found at www.drupal.org, whilst country-specific websites offering support for developers are also available (in the UK, visit www.drupal.org.uk).

TypePad

TypePad Micro is a free-to-use micro blog that can be linked to Facebook and Twitter, providing a platform to post short messages and display images and links. If you want a more sophisticated blog, there are a number of packages with monthly subscriptions starting at $8.95, although 14-day free trial versions are available. For further details, see www.typepad.com.

Online Blog Services

There are a number of blogs that can be quickly set up online and the majority of them are free. Search for them through Yahoo! or Google. Websites including www.blogger.com, www.thoughts.com and www.blog.com can all host free blogs. Generally, the setting up of an online blog involves registering an account and setting preferences. The advantage of

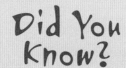

Did You Know?

According to Wikipedia, on 16 February 2011, there were over 156 million public blogs on the internet!

using such a service is your blog may be automatically listed in a number of directories, which helps to attract readers.

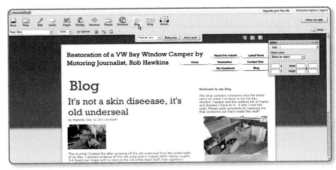

Online Websites With Blogs

If you have used an online website design service to create a website, such as the one outlined earlier in this chapter, then it may include a

Above: Most online web design services include a blog, which is straightforward to set up and as easy to manage as your website.

blog. This can be added to your website online and permissions set to allow other people to leave comments. Your own posts to the blog can be made via the online website design page.

Create a Blog Online With Blogger

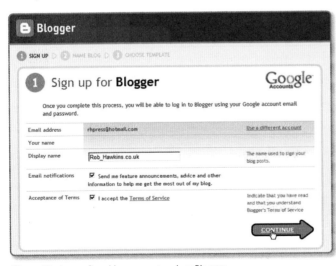

Above: Signing up for a blog account such as Blogger makes use of a Google account for registration.

Setting up a blog online with a free service such as Blogger is one of the quickest ways to become an online author. The following step-by-step guide shows what's involved:

✅ **Register**: The first stage in creating an online blog is to register with the service that is providing it. In the case of Blogger, a

Above: A blogger's profile can be edited to make it personal, adding details concerning hobbies and interests and photographs.

Google account can be used to register. Next, the blog needs to be established with a display name and your email address for correspondence.

 Your profile: You may want to create a profile for yourself, adding a photograph and details about your hobbies and interests. This helps anyone viewing the blog to find out more about you and why you wanted to create the blog in the first place.

 Blog title and address: A suitable title for your blog is essential, along with an easy-to-remember address. Most providers of free blog sites will generate an address that includes their details. You may find many addresses have already been used.

 Layout and design: Once you've established the settings for your blog,

Above: A title helps to describe your blog. An address needs to be easy to remember, but may have already been used by someone else.

you're ready to choose a design, then start blogging. You may want to start off with a post and notify a number of people, then wait for the comments.

Blog Publicity

There are a number of methods of publicizing your blog and ensuring more readers visit the site. These include the following:

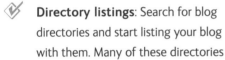

Above: Blogs don't need to be endless lists of text. They can use colourful designs and illustrations.

 Directory listings: Search for blog directories and start listing your blog with them. Many of these directories are free, although paid listings usually include photos and priority placements in search results. Free listings may take longer to be included as they often have to be manually checked.

 Reciprocal links: Find the websites associated with your blog and ask to swap links, whereby you display their website as a link on your blog and they display your blog on their website.

 Social networking: Join social networks including Twitter and Facebook and establish a link to your blog. Find other people who are interested in your subject and start creating your own publicity.

Forums: Find any relevant forums and see if you can include a link to your blog.

Hot Tip
Regularly update your blog to make sure you keep your audience interested.

Pricing Options

○ Featured »» PERMANENT, Top Category listing, 5 deep links, 24 hour approval, ONLY 10 per category, PHOTO of site added
○ Regular »» PERMANENT, Sub Category listing, 3 deep links, 3 day approval, PHOTO added
● Reciprocal »» 1 year active only, sub Category listing, 0 additional links, 30 day approval, Reciprocal Link REQUIRED, NO Photo

*Title: VW Camper restoration

*URL: http://vwcamper.moonfrut.com/#/bl

Description: Restoration and ongoing modifications of a 1976 VW Camper owned by Rob Hawkins
Limit: 422

META Keywords: VW, Campervan, Bay Window

META Description: Restoration and ongoing modifications of a 1976 VW Camper owned by Rob Hawkins
Limit: 172

*Your Name: Rob Hawkins

*Your Email: rhpress@hotmail.com

*Category: Cars & Autos
Change category

Reciprocal Link URL: http://vwcamper.moonfruit.com/#/bl

To validate the reciprocal link please include the following HTML code in the page at the URL specified above, before submiting this form:

<a href="http://www.bloghints.com/">BLOG DIRECTORY, Submit blog free, Promote Blog, Best directory</a>

Above: Listing your blog with a directory can help to increase its exposure and hopefully attract more readers.

Making Money From a Blog

A blog won't directly make you money from posting comments and keeping a diary of events, but it is currently one of the most useful marketing tools for attracting an audience and generating publicity. Consequently, it can generate money by the following methods:

☑ **Affiliate advertising**:
If you can include affiliate advertising on your blog, this can be used to generate income. The products or services offered by affiliate advertisers can be mentioned in your blog, but be careful, there's a fine line between being independent and being seen as favouring your advertisers with advertorial.

☑ **Click-through links**: Whilst most blogs can include links, some can be set to monitor who clicks on those links. This is especially useful if you want to prove to a potential advertiser that a link to them in the text of your blog generates visitors to their website. If you can direct enough traffic and prove it, there are grounds for charging for click-throughs.

☑ **Specialist status**: If you provide a service, such as tuition or consultancy, then your blog can be used to help promote your area of expertise and lead to bookings. From another angle, a blog that perceives you as a specialist can lead to television and radio interviews and other similar appearances within the mainstream media.

☑ **Link to sales**: If you sell particular products, these can be reviewed or mentioned in your blog along with links to buy them.

Other Website Features

A website needs interesting, relevant and varied content to entice visitors to keep coming back. There are a number of features that can be incorporated into a website to help it look both professional and useful.

Guestbook

A guestbook or visitor log allows people viewing your website to leave comments and acknowledge they have looked at your website. Depending on the type of guestbook, comments can be left by anyone or limited to people you know. The method of adding a guestbook depends on how your website has been created and whether your website host allows guestbooks to be included. Some online web design services include a guestbook and there are free guestbook hosting services, which can be linked to your website or hosted within it.

Above: Setting up a free online guestbook with organizations such as Bravenet is straightforward and requires little technical knowledge.

Latest News

Keeping a website current with up-to-the minute information can become very time consuming. One of the most effective forms of making a website seem current is to display the latest news. Thankfully, you don't have to look through online

Hot Tip
Avoid malicious and irrelevant messages by setting restrictions on your guestbook and frequently checking it.

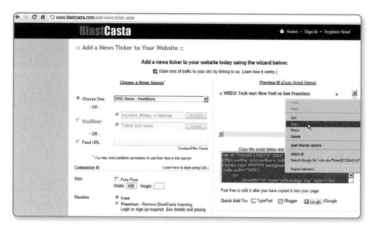

Above: The latest news can be displayed as a simple headline using code copied from websites such as www.blastcasta.com.

news websites and create your own news. Instead, a news link can be included, which allows the latest news to be displayed on your website. The news is added as a link and embedded into a web page.

Search Engine Boost or Ban

Some search engines rank a website according to the number of external links coming into it and the quantity of regularly updated and relevant content. Including the latest news in your home page can help with some search engines, but sadly, it can also have a negative effect as more and more websites use news feed services – now that news feeds have become a known SEO winner, some search engine experts are recommending to avoid using them because search engines may count this against you in their ranking if the rest of the website is not news related. It's worthwhile looking into this before adding news to your website.

Voting and Polls

> **Hot Tip**
> Free online news services include www.rssfeedreader.com, which can be added to your website.

The internet has become a popular platform for people to express their opinions. Voting and polls are also useful marketing tools, enabling competitions to be run where voters have to register their details to win a prize. This approach can be used for a variety of purposes, ranging from straightforward competitions to voting and deciding on the progress of a project.

Voting Success Story for Xbox and Tornado

When Forza Motorsport 4 for the Xbox was launched in 2011, the promoters built one of the cars featured in the game and gave it away as a competition prize. A Ford GT40 replica called the Tornado TS40 was constructed over five days in a West London shopping centre and live-streamed video footage of the build was available to view online. Viewers could vote on the specification of the car, including choosing the wheels, the front body style, shock absorbers, stripes and brakes. Over 14,000 votes were received and interest in the Tornado TS40 and Forza Motorsport 4 was boosted.

Right: The launch of Forza Motorsport 4 for the Xbox was heavily promoted by building one of the game's race cars, giving it away as a competition prize and allowing people to vote online regarding its specification.

Product or Site Searching

Including a search box on your website can help visitors locate items within your website or elsewhere on the internet. A search box can be included by copy-pasting the relevant code from another website, or by visiting a website such as www.freefind.com, www.fusionbot.com and many others that can be found using a search engine (search for 'free search box for my website').

Earn Money From a Search Box

Google can provide a search box where results can be customized to help list advertisers that pay for click-throughs and other marketing methods.

Hot Tip

The price-comparison website Pricerunner offers an AdRunner Widget, which enables visitors to your website to compare products and earns you money if they buy.

Google Ads can also be displayed alongside search results to boost the advertising revenue. This method of advertising is particularly useful for a review or hobby/interest website, where businesses can promote their products through search results.

Left: Website www.citycottage.co.uk uses an events calendar from Eventbrite to list its future courses.

Online Calendar

A simple calendar showing important events, such as shows, product release dates and other relevant information can help to attract visitors to return. A calendar can be something as simple as an image, list or table included in your website. Alternatively, third-party calendars can be incorporated, which can be customized with links to events and entries. This can help to attract advertisers where they can add their own dates and monitor click-throughs.

Linking to Facebook and Twitter

Include a link through to your postings on Facebook, Twitter and other social networking websites to help increase publicity and establish a wider audience. Encourage visitors to your website to join these social networking websites to keep in contact with you and receive the latest updates. If you're running a business, tempt them with the latest offers and competitions. Many of these sites are linked through to mobile devices such as smartphones, enabling updates to be instantly received.

Email Forms

Make contacting you as easy as possible, so instead of simply displaying an email address, provide feedback and enquiry forms with encouraging questions to complete. This can help with market research: for instance, ask visitors how they found your website. If you're running a hobby or interest-based website, ask for suggestions for topics to explore, which may in turn help with advertising. If you're selling items through a website, offer forms for enquiries, complaints and other effective categories of communication.

Spam Forms

The danger of offering online forms for visitors to complete comes from automatic programs that scan your website, complete any forms and fill your inbox with junk messages. This can be avoided by including a security question, which cannot be answered by such programs. Many forms display some difficult-to-read text as an image that must be entered into a box to submit the form. Other forms display a simple mathematical calculation that you have to correctly answer to submit the form.

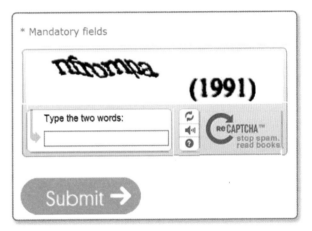

Above: Online forms can be inundated with automated spam, but this can be reduced with a question box like this, which cannot be answered by a spam-generating program.

Live Chat

Instant online communication with visitors to your website is an effective method of publicity, but it can be time consuming. It can be used to review a product, provide instructions or guidance, or answer queries. There are a number of methods of running a live chat, including the following:

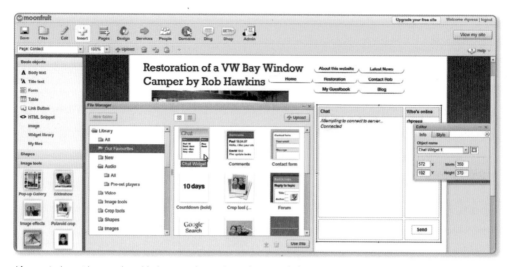

Above: A chat widget can be added to an online website design package such as Moonfruit. With this one, visitors must register and log in to post comments and questions.

Messenger service: One of the cheapest methods is to rely upon a third-party messenger service such as Yahoo! or MSN. This requires people to log in to these services and accept invitations, which helps to provide security and privacy, but doesn't allow an instant audience to be generated. It is a useful free method of customer support and if the equipment is available, it can be conducted via a webcam.

Live chat: This is becoming a popular method of instant communication with software packages that can be added to a website. Subscription services are more flexible and easier to set up, but there are some free live-chat packages, which can in some cases be incorporated with messenger services.

Add a widget: Many online website design services can include a 'chat widget', which allows instant messages to be posted. If you're logged in, you can respond to them immediately. In some cases, visitors must register and log in to be able to post comments and questions.

Successful Website Marketing

The key to a successful money-making website is to ensure it is effectively marketed. This involves several methodologies, which need to be thoroughly researched to ensure they're successful and don't waste your time and money.

Search Engines

The traditional starting point for publicizing a website is to register it with a number of search engines and allow them to assess and rank it. This can take a long time if you don't pay for the assessment. You simply submit your details and wait. If you're willing to pay for being listed with a search engine, then there are a number of privileges to be had, including a faster assessment, being included in featured search results (a separate listing at the side or top of the screen) and being included in other websites which use the search engine.

Above: There is a wide range of free search engine submission services that will submit your website to the most popular search engines. This one is operated by www.submitexpress.com and works with over 70 search engines.

Keywords and Meta Tags

One of the traditional methods of successful listings through search engines is to ensure you have relevant words displayed on your home page, which can link you through to the typical search questions people will use in a search engine. So if you run a flower shop in Amsterdam, make sure you display the words 'flower shop, Amsterdam, Holland, Netherlands' on the home page. It's also useful to add these to the description, keywords and title of your website. However, many search engines look deeper into your website to assess its content, so don't think this alone will provide good search results.

Relevant Searches and Click-throughs

Many search engines assess what people look for and what they choose to help rank their results listings. Consequently, whilst you may find your website is at the top of the search results one week, if nobody clicks through to it, you may find it's listed further down the following week.

Crawlers and Spiders

Search engines trawl the internet to find information using software called a crawler or spider (Google's is called a Googlebot). The programs follow page links and attempt to index information. There are lots of websites offering spider simulators, which will assess your website and reveal what results can be found (search for 'spider simulator').

Directories and Listings

Dedicated directories such as www.yell.com, www.yellowpages.com, www.118.com and www.thomsonlocal.com are recognized and popular methods of finding businesses and specialists ranging from a local plumber to a restaurant or hotel. Before applying for a listing, it's worthwhile searching for similar businesses using these directories to see if this type of listing is effective. In most cases, a fee is applicable

Left: Directory listings websites are a useful source for registering your website and business.

(although free basic listings are often available), but a well-placed listing can often be more direct than a search engine and more effective.

Above: Many directory listings are free to join, although the more you pay, the more exposure you receive.

Price Comparison Sites

If you sell products through your website, then look at the various price comparison websites to see if it's worthwhile listing with such sites. In some cases, you'll be charged at a cost per click (CPC) rate every time someone clicks through to your website. These websites also offer additional display advertising on their pages.

Reciprocal Links

Sharing links between different websites is an effective method of increasing the popularity and awareness of all the websites involved. This method works not only because your website has a greater chance of being visited from other sites, but also because search engines analyze the number of links you have on your website to help rank its popularity and relevance. Try to

Above: The De Havilland Motor Company has developed a recreation of the Ferrari Dino and used Facebook to catalogue its progress. This free publicity proved to be extremely popular and only required the frequent posting of comments and photographs.

establish links to any website that is relevant to yours, such as forums, owners clubs, advertisers, specialists and blogs. Many websites include a page of links with relevant website addresses, logos and other illustrations, but it may also be useful to swap advertisements and place them throughout your website.

Social Networks

Many businesses have created an audience of followers through social network sites including Facebook and Twitter. Anyone involved is kept up to date with the latest information and events, which helps to publicize a website. Most websites include a 'Follow us on Facebook' or equivalent link, which when clicked on, opens the respective social network and allows the visitor to log in and join in.

Publicity Campaigns

Whilst the methodologies of ensuring as many people as possible know about your website are essential to creating visitors, another aspect of marketing is to find a way of enticing them to visit. This involves generating new publicity, including the following:

New products: If you're selling items, announce the arrival of new products to ensure everyone concerned knows about it.

Competitions: Running a competition is a relatively easy thing to do. It's a useful exercise for advertisers to offer a free product or service in return for some potential customers. Similarly, if you sell items or provide a service, it's an effective method of finding new customers.

Discounts/bargains: Many selling websites have clearance and discount pages, which attract lots of visitors and are an effective source of new publicity.

Publicity Campaign Techniques

Getting the message out to the internet to explain about new products, competitions, discounts and clearance items requires several different campaign techniques. Most businesses use the following methods:

Email: Seller websites offer mailing lists for customers and regularly send updates concerning discounts (including discount vouchers) and clearance items in the form of an email newsletter or notice.

Third-party emails: There are several websites that find discount vouchers, discount codes and competitions. Inform these sources and they will do the work for you.

Above: Custom bodywork specialist and painter John Pinder has a large following on Facebook, which he finds provides successful publicity campaigns when he offers discounts.

Facebook/Twitter: Publicity is easy to build up on social network sites, whether it's the countdown to the release of a new product or the progress of a launch or new service. People want to know and be a part of it.

Blog: Just like social network sites, a blog can build up the excitement of something new.

 Forums: Find the forums that are relevant to your website and keep posting the latest news and events.

Home page news: Make sure your home page contains your latest news and it's easy to see. This helps with search engine assessment and ensures visitors spot your latest developments straight away.

Above: Press releases should be straight to the point with clear information, including product descriptions, pricing and contact details. This email press release from Laser Tools is ideal, and the text and images can be copied to make a news item.

Professional Publicity

The media is always looking for newsworthy material. Whilst large organizations employ a press team (in house or an external specialist), generating media publicity is all about finding the right contacts and emailing them with breaking news and exciting developments. Most magazines, websites and other media have someone responsible for creating news and they are often only too keen to accept press releases in the form of an email.

Hot Tip
Images for press releases can be stored online at websites including Flickr and PhotoBucket, which are easy to access and download.

Measuring the Success of a Website

The ultimate success of a website is based on how much money you make from it, but in order to increase what you make from it, you need to know whether its publicity is effective and if visitors are being correctly directed to the goods you're selling, the services you're offering and the affiliate advertising you want them to click on. The following pages show how to assess the success of your website.

Rank Your Website

There are a number of free online tools that help to assess your website in the same way a search engine will check through it. Page Rank (www.prchecker.info) is a free service that checks Google's page ranking. A button can also be added to your website to enable you to quickly check a page. Other free online checking tools aim to replicate the activity of a spider or crawler (explained in the previous section of this chapter) and provide rating results. These include Alex, DMOZ, Domain Age and Yahoo!

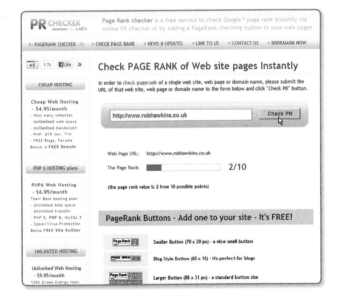

Above: PR Checker enables a website to be page ranked according to the techniques employed by Google.

SEO Success Story

Paul Malish is the founder and owner of a number of successful UK-based online city guides (for example, www.leeds-city-guide.com) and a guide to privately owned rental properties and holiday villas in Florida, USA, focused on the Orlando area (www.orlando-villa-guide.com). By strategically employing effective search engine optimization techniques his websites are uniquely positioned to maximize and capitalize upon the revenue streams that drive the business. As he explains, 'It is precisely because of our hard-won position as the number-one ranked website in Google's search results for many of our relevant search terms that our business model is so successful. Duplicate or cloned copies of our websites would be unable to achieve the same success and levels of revenue without employing highly effective search engine optimization techniques. Indeed, many potential competitors have tried such an approach [mimicing his websites closely] over the years only to fail and then subsequently disappear completely offline. A good analogy might be the difference between opening a shop on a small remote Pacific Island, where there are no customers, and opening the same shop on, say, Oxford Street in central London. The amount of potential revenue generated is driven by the volume of the traffic and the perceived worth of any advertising opportunities.'

Search Engine Optimization (SEO)

Search engine optimization is a process of improving the visibility of a website in search engines via its search results. It looks at aspects of a search engine, including how it works, how it assesses websites, what people look for, the words typed into search engines and which search engines are preferred by a website's target audience. Consequently, there are now specialists and consultants who offer to help improve search results for a website, either as a service on its own or as part of a marketing and website design package.

DIY SEO

Use a number of search engines and look for keywords that should relate to your website. See if your website appears in the search results listings. If it doesn't, find out why other websites are more successful. Are their keywords more relevant? Look at their pages to see if there are any aspects that help with their ranking.

> ## Hot Tip
> Assessment of the success of your website includes looking at your competitors and determining why they are better.

Analytics Software

Software such as Google Analytics helps to calculate the number of visitors to your website and what they do when they get there. Google's version is free to use and all you need to do is register and copy some tracking code into your website's pages to allow the visitor analysis to be recorded. The type of useful information provided by analytics software usually includes the following:

 Bounce rate: The number of visitors who arrive at your website and leave immediately. This can reflect incorrect search results via a search engine or a misleading title and description for your website.

Above: Google Analytics is free to use and helps to understand visitor behaviour on your website.

✅ **Conversion rate**: The number of visitors who do what you wanted them to do – make a purchase, click on affiliate advertising. Rates can be low. For instance, expect a 2–3% conversion rate for a selling website.

✅ **Target pages**: If some pages in your website are more important than others (items for sale or affiliate advertisements), the proportion of visited target pages in relation to visitors helps to identify if you've correctly positioned these essential pages.

✅ **Site search data**: If you have a search box that provides search results for the products you sell or the content in your website, then analytics software can reveal what people are searching for, which helps to identify products you don't have and calculate percentage sales from search results. You may find your search box isn't helping at all.

✅ **Visitor location**: Calculating where your visitors are located is essential, especially if you're selling products and cannot supply to particular countries. Similarly, you may find you want to translate your pages for overseas visitors.

> ## Hot Tip
> Analytics software can be found at Piwik, Snoop, BBClone and Woopra.

Website Host Data

Some website hosting services can provide data on who is visiting your website, where they are located, what time they visit and how long they stay on your website. This can help determine when you may want to run live chats, post blogs, update the site and provide support. There are also a number of websites offering free traffic reports for your own website.

Compete Analysis

Compete collates the internet activity of two million users in the USA to determine which websites they visit and how they find them. This information is available to view for free for your own website and others. Go to www.compete.com and enter a website address to see if any data is available. This is also a useful exercise for assessing your competitors and looking at websites you can use, such as classifieds, price comparisons, eBay and Amazon.

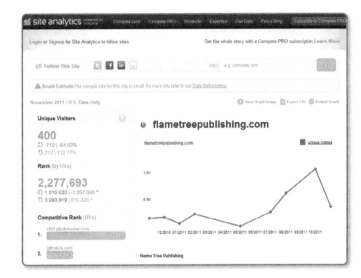

Above: Online statistics from Site Analytics at www.compete.com can provide a calculation of unique monthly visitors to a website based on a poll of two million USA internet users.

Above: Website visitor statistics from Site Analytics at www.compete.com can be useful for assessing websites you may want to use to sell products, such as eBay.

Payment Methods For a Website

If you're selling something through your website, then you need to make sure you have a safe and secure method of receiving payments. The following pages provide an outline of some of the payment methods available.

PayPal

PayPal has become a recognized and popular means of making payments, thanks to worldwide selling websites such as eBay. PayPal members register a credit or debit card with their respective

PayPal account, then they can make and receive payments. Any payments that are received are charged a commission of between 1.4–3.4% in most cases, along with a £0.20 or $0.30 transaction fee. PayPal provides a range of services that can be incorporated into your website to allow visitors to purchase and pay for items (for example, Express Checkout). When it comes to paying, PayPal deals with this, then returns the customer to your website.

Google Checkout

Google Checkout is becoming an increasingly popular method of payment and is in direct competition with PayPal. It follows a similar payment method to PayPal, allowing a member's details to include a credit or debit card. Fees are also comparable to PayPal.

eBay Shops and Amazon

If you're selling items via your website, but also have them listed through a selling website such as eBay or Amazon, then you can link through to these websites to complete purchases and payments. This often appeals to some customers, who trust recognized worldwide sellers such as eBay and Amazon.

Above: Some retailers use eBay to handle specific items. Worldwide classic car parts supplier Moss uses eBay for its lightly damaged items.

Credit and Debit Card Payments

There are a number of specialists who can complete credit and debit card payments for you through your website. Popular organizations include WorldPay (www.worldpay.com) and SecureTrading (www.securetrading.com), who can offer everything from handling payments to setting up a shopping cart. Fees vary and many packages are designed for large volume sales.

E-commerce Packages

Setting up a website to sell goods can be a logistical nightmare, with issues concerning listing items, cataloguing, updating prices, payment methods and all the finer details that are required to successfully run a selling website with an online shopping cart. Consequently, a number of website hosting services have started to offer e-commerce packages where they look after everything. All you have to do is supply the details concerning the goods you want to sell. Costs vary and are usually competitive with other e-commerce methods mentioned in this chapter.

Other Money-making Ideas

Internet Consultancy

There are still thousands of businesses who want to transfer their trade on to the internet, but have been put off by high costs and vague estimations of how much they can make. There's clearly an opportunity for putting your own skills to use and helping such businesses on a small scale. Similarly, many businesses have a website that has never been assessed or improved upon, which is a perfect opportunity for offering your services.

Make a Website

As shown in the previous chapter, creating a website doesn't have to be a complicated process. On a basic level, a website can be created for free using an online web design service. With sufficient practice, a single page website can be created in a few minutes. When you become proficient in creating websites using this method, there's the scope to be able to offer this to businesses, but make it clear what the limitations are:

Above: In chapter five (Make a Website), we showed how to create a website using a free online design and hosting service such as Moonfruit. This can lead to a whole new career designing sites for other businesses.

✅ **Cutting costs**: You can create a simple website, which helps to keep costs low. Sophisticated websites with drop-down menus, video and shopping carts take time to develop and that is where costs can escalate.

The basics: Encourage the development of a basic website at the start to allow the business time to assess its success. In the future, it can move on to a more complicated website if necessary.

 Be honest: Outline your skill level, what you can do and your limitations. If you don't know how to develop a shopping cart, be honest about how far you can go with the creation of a website.

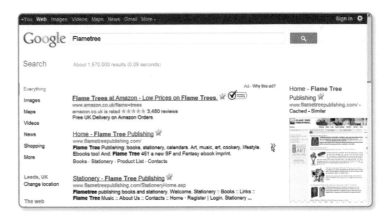

Hot Tip

Many web-hosting services offer a range of packages, which can be used for setting up e-commerce and other business-related activities.

Website Marketing

A small army of internet specialists offering to improve the popularity of your website has emerged in the last 10 years. There's no dark art to improving the flow of traffic to a website and most of the techniques are outlined in this book in the previous chapter. Once you've practised them yourself, you can quickly be in a position to help others with your knowledge.

Website Assessment

Many businesses don't have the time to assess their website. Offering a straightforward method of assessing a website can include the following:

 Search results: How easy is it to find the website using different search criteria?

Above: Analysing a customer's website can include assessment of search engine results.

Home page: Does the home page appear quickly and does it convey the correct message? Try viewing the home page on friends' computers to assess its loading time and whether it fits into the screen.

Target pages: Are the important pages easy to find? If a website demonstrates a product and requires visitors to contact the seller and place an order, are these pages easy to find with relevant menus or buttons on the screen?

Layout and colours: Assess the overall design of the website. Is it viewable for anyone who is colour blind? Are the choice of colours and fonts easy on the eyes?

Clarity: Does the website provide a clear indication of its structure and content? Test the website on various friends to see if they understand its content and observe how they navigate around it.

Competitors: Assess any competitors' websites and note what is better compared to the website you are analyzing.

Analytical results: Analytics software was outlined in the previous chapter and can provide some useful information concerning ranking, keywords and other essential ingredients that make a website successful.

> ## Hot Tip
>
> See www.clicknwork.com for opportunities to work from home via the internet.

Search Engine Expert

There is sufficient information on the internet to explain how to improve a website's position in a search engine's results list. With enough practice, this knowledge can be put to use and offered as part of a consultancy service to help improve a website. Most of the information outlined in chapter five (Make a Website) will help to improve the popularity of a website and increase its ranking with search engines.

Website Enhancements

One of the methods of improving the popularity of a website is to include several features that attract visitors, such as a blog, forum and accounts with various social networking websites. These methods can be time consuming and seemingly non-productive for a business, but they are essential internet marketing tools that will invariably be offered by marketing specialists who'll operate them for a customer to help improve their website's popularity.

Hot Tip

Consolidate all your social network services into one with a social network aggregation platform, such as www.sociagg.com.

Success Story of Social Marketing

Canadian-born Mari Smith grew up in Scotland and now lives in California, USA, where she has become a guru within the field of social marketing, offering everything from consultancy to seminars. She has also written a number of books. Mari was all set to become a motivational speaker in 1998. The following year she moved to the USA and soon started to specialize in relationship marketing, email marketing and web copy. In 2007, she became immersed in social media and soon realized the power of the emerging and fast-growing sites including Facebook. Nowadays, you can find Mari on Facebook, Twitter, LinkedIn, Google+ and YouTube. She also has her own website at www.marismith.com.

Write a Book

The internet initially opened the marketplace for books, thanks largely to Amazon who slashed prices. However, the book market has evolved and now it's easier than ever to publish your own work and make money from it. The following section reveals some of the websites and services that can help you make a living as an author.

Book Types

A book can be created and sold online in a variety of formats, which all generate different forms of income. Here are some of the popular approaches:

 Apps: Apple's iPad and iPhone and similar tablets and smartphones can be used to read a book via applications (apps for short), which can be downloaded from a source such as Apple's iBookstore that takes a 30% cut of the selling price.

 E-books for e-book readers or 'e-readers': Amazon's Kindle is a dedicated reader for electronic books (e-books) and can be connected to the internet to purchase and download books from Kindle's online store. Amazon takes 65% of the selling price. Similar readers include Nook (from Barnes & Noble) and Kobo.

- **E-books for computers**: A computer connected to the internet can be used to read electronic books using freely available software.

- **Paper on demand**: There are a number of online book publishers who allow you to upload your book, sell it through their website and others such as Amazon, and receive a percentage or all of the profits (after the cost price of the book has been deducted). See www.lulu.com and www.blurb.com for more details.

- **Make it yourself**: Create your own electronic book and sell it via your own website or via a relevant selling site. Lulu.com can do this for you, but will include their branding. Alternatively, create a PDF using Microsoft Word or a PDF creator and providing the format is correct, you have your own e-book for distribution.

- **Find a publisher**: This is often one of the most difficult approaches to publishing a book, but can be more financially rewarding if a fixed fee is agreed (some books are only paid on royalties).

Lulu.com

Lulu.com was established in 2002 and specializes in open publishing, with approximately 20,000 titles added each month and over one million writers. They offer their free service to authors in exchange for a small percentage of profits from each sale. Lulu provides anyone with the ability to publish books, e-books, mini-books, photo books, calendars, cookbooks

Hot Tip

Visit www.fastpencil.com for lots of information on becoming an online author and using FastPencil's professional services.

and travel books. A book or similar publication can be uploaded as a text file with images or as a PDF. Lulu then converts this into a book format and calculates the cost of making each book. It is then the author's decision to determine a selling price of which Lulu takes a 20% cut of the profit. Publications and other material are available online at Lulu.com and through third-party sellers including Amazon and Kindle.

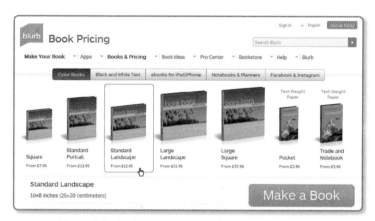

Blurb.com

Blurb.com is similar to Lulu.com, offering a book publication service. You can calculate how much a book will cost to manufacture, then decide on a selling price. Blurb doesn't take a percentage of the profit, but charges a processing fee every time you are paid – payments are monthly and the fee is £1, $1

Above: Online book makers such as Blurb provide a price for how much your book will cost to manufacture, enabling you to set a cover price and make some profit from each sale.

or whatever your country's currency. Blurb provides an online book creator, but also has downloadable software to enable you to design your book (there's also a professional version with a plug-in for Adobe InDesign).

Createspace.com

Owned by Amazon, Createspace.com offers free and paid-for book publishing services with on-demand printed books. Your book can be created online by uploading it as a Word document or PDF, then viewed using Interior Reviewer software, checked for printing errors and trimmed if necessary. Books can be created in electronic format for the Kindle and in paper format. Both can be sold through Amazon, including your own Amazon eStore. There's even an online calculator, so you can see how much money you can make based on the size of your book, the number of pages and the cover price.

Calculating Your Royalty
- List Price (set by you)
- − Our Share
- = **Your Royalty**

Need more information?
Setting your book's list price
How we calculate our share

Royalty Calculator*
Use the royalty calculator to figure out how much you'll make every time your book is manufactured.

		eStore		Amazon.com		Expanded Distribution
		Standard	☆ Pro	Standard	☆ Pro	☆ Pro
List Price	15.00					
Interior Type	Black and Whi ▾					
Trim Size	5" x 8" ▾	**Your Royalty**				
Number of Pages	200	$6.50	$8.75	$3.50	$5.75	$2.75
	Calculate	**Our Share**				
		$8.50 Details	$6.25 Details	$11.50 Details	$9.25 Details	$12.25 Details

* Figures generated by this tool are for estimation purposes only. Your actual royalty will be calculated when you set up your book.

Above: Amazon's www.createspace.com enables you to publish your own book and sell it through a number of Amazon-related outlets. There's even an online calculator so you can see how much money you will make.

Book Promotion

Once you've published a book online, there's no sitting back and waiting for the money to start flooding in. The best way to ensure sales of your book is to become involved in marketing it. This can involve the following ideas: ·

- **Book website**: Create a website about your book, explaining how you wrote it, what inspired you and any other details which help to build a picture that persuades people to buy it. Include a link to enable visitors to buy your book.

- **Blog your book**: Join a blog or include one in your website that talks about your book. You may want to run a blog whilst writing it or whilst writing a sequel.

- **Radio style**: Include weekly or monthly audio files in your website, introducing readings from your book to tempt listeners into buying it. This can also help to promote your profile as you can explain characters and plots within your book.

Social networking: Everyone likes to be friends with an author, so social network sites including Facebook, LinkedIn and Google+ can be used to find people interested in literature who may want to become involved with your book. Such a network can become an instant customer base for future books.

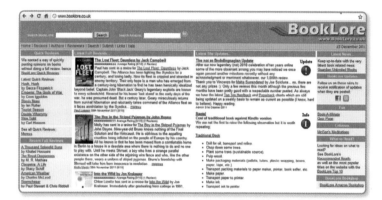

 Book websites: Find as many literature-related websites as possible and make sure you can publicize your book through them. Offer interviews, advice and other activities to become involved.

Above: Book review websites such as www.booklore.co.uk display reviews from readers with marks out of 10. Books can be found by author and reviewers can also be searched.

 Local book stores: If you have some local independent book stores, find out if they are willing to stock your books on a sale-or-return basis. If so, you may want to buy a bulk quantity of your books (these are often cheaper) and leave them with these shop(s).

 Competitions and offers: Can you give away a few of your books as competition prizes for a magazine or website?

Literary reviews: Contact magazines and websites that cover the subject concerned with your book and enquire about a review. If they are willing, make sure a book is delivered and follow it up afterwards.

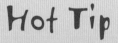

Hot Tip

ClickBank.com can sell your e-books and pays commission on selling other people's e-books.

Savings, Discounts and Deals

Making money on the internet isn't just about generating income, it's also about finding the offers, discounts and deals that can save you money, and there are plenty of them out there. There are numerous websites that trawl the internet for special offers, but you can also find them yourself.

Discount Codes and Offers

Search the internet for discount codes and you'll find a vast assortment of websites offering links to discounts on the major retail websites. Most of these can already be found via the relevant retailer's website, but these discount websites help to gather numerous offers together.

Groupon Savings

Launched in November 2008, Groupon has gained worldwide popularity by featuring discounted deals on anything from a meal to a holiday or car service. The deals are applicable to the country you live in and your nearest city or town. Headquartered in Chicago, USA, Groupon now covers 46 countries and has roughly 10,000 employees working in offices

Above: Deal website Groupon offers savings on a wide range of purchases, from a meal in a local restaurant to a holiday abroad.

around the world. Discounted deals offered through Groupon have to be bought online and the customer then arranges the booking. For instance, if a Groupon deal is available on a particular hotel, you have to purchase this online, then contact the hotel to make a booking.

Groupon Money Makers

You can earn extra cash through Groupon by recommending offers to friends, relatives and colleagues via email, Facebook, Twitter and other social networks. If someone buys a deal which you've recommended to them, you receive a Groupon credit (£6 in the UK) which can be used against a future Groupon deal. This entitles you to an even greater discount on your next deal – or you could even have it for nothing!

Forum and Club Offers

If you are involved in a forum or club concerning a hobby or interest, you may be able to get together with a few members and agree to purchase items in bulk. All you need to do is contact a relevant supplier and see what discount they are willing to offer based on a specific volume of sales, then post a request on the relevant forum asking for interested buyers to contact you.

Hot Tip

If you regularly visit a restaurant or hotel, ask if they have a mailing list for offers and make sure you join it.

Cashback and Discounts

There are a number of websites that offer cashback and discounted offers from major retailers and similar businesses. Joining such a website allows you to shop online and make use of these offers. There are also printable discount vouchers for use in restaurants and high-street stores. In most cases, all you need to do is register with a particular cashback website, find an offer you like through their website and click on it to start shopping online with discounted prices or cashback offers (the same applies to finding printable discount vouchers). Popular websites include Quidco.com, Topcashback.co.uk, Quickrewards.net and BigCrumbs.com.

Above: Find cashback and discounts via websites such as www.bigcrumbs.com for purchases of goods and services.

Delayed Discounts and Cashback

In most cases, the discount or cashback received on a purchase through a website such as Quidco or Topcashback isn't deducted from the selling price of the goods or service you purchase. Instead, it becomes a credit and is held by the cashback website for a few days or weeks to allow time for returns. Eventually, this money is paid to you via a credit/debit card, bank payment, PayPal account or gift vouchers. In some cases, a minimum amount of credit has to be accrued, £15 or $20, before a payment is made to help reduce transaction costs.

Did You Know?

Most cashback and discount websites receive commission for your purchases and pass on a percentage of this to you. This is how they make their money.

Mobile Apps

Mobile devices such as smartphones, personal digital assistants (PDAs) and tablet computers have created a whole new market for applications ranging from amusing sounds to useful drawing and note-taking tools. These applications are often created by amateur programmers using readily available software and sold through specific websites. The following section reveals how you can develop your own applications and earn money.

App Operating Systems

Smartphones and other mobile devices use a specific operating system, just like a PC uses Windows or Linux, or an Apple Mac computer uses Mac OS X. These operating systems are also referred to as platforms. The common ones are as follows:

 Google Android: This is an open-source operating system, derived from Linux and installed on a wide variety of devices ranging from video cameras and digital compasses to GPS and smartphones. It is owned by Google Inc.

 iOS: Apple's operating system for its range of devices (iPhone, iPad and IPod Touch), which is derived from the Mac OS X.

Palm OS: This was one of the earliest operating systems for mobile devices and has evolved over the years with new names including Garnet OS, Access Linux and more recently, webOS. Commonly found on Hewlett Packard devices because webOS is owned by HP.

Blackberry OS: Used on a wide range of Blackberry mobile devices, which are all owned by the Canadian-based business, Research In Motion (RIM). This operating system will be replaced by Blackberry BBX.

Symbian OS: A popular operating system for Nokia, Motorola, Samsung and Sony Ericsson mobile devices.

Samsung Bada: One of the newest operating systems and developed by Samsung Electronics for its range of mobile devices, enabling many feature phones to become smartphones. Applications are sold through the Samsung Apps store.

Did You Know?

A software development kit or SDK (also known as a devkit) is a set of programs used to create an application.

Windows Phone: Developed by Microsoft, this operating system provides full integration with services such as Xbox Live, Bing, Facebook and Google accounts.

Developing an App

There are a number of considerations before developing an app for a mobile device. These issues may have you running round in circles as decisions change and problems arise. A good starting point is to arm yourself with several ideas for apps, then do some research into the following:

Above: Apple's App Store has over half a million apps for the iPhone and other Apple devices.

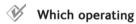

Does it already exist? Find out whether your app has already been created. Search through a variety of apps stores for it.

Find a SDK: A software development kit (SDK for short) is required to be able to produce your app. Some of these are free, whereas others incur a fee.

Which operating system? Determining which operating system will run your app may be difficult. It all depends on other factors, such as the devices you want to target, whether you can acquire an SDK and where you can sell your app.

Where to sell: Find out where your app can be sold. This is often based upon which operating system you choose. For instance, if you develop an app for the iPhone, you may find it's best to sell it through Apple's App Store.

SDK downloads

If you are familiar with programming languages, then you may be able to download a suitable software development kit and start creating your own apps using a PC or Apple Mac. Android's SDK can be used on a Windows or Linux based PC, or an Apple Mac running OS X and downloaded via www.developer.android.com. Apps developers for iPhones and other Apple devices can find the SDK at www.developer.apple.com.

Online Apps Creators

There are a number of websites offering the free online creation of apps, but these are often not as easy to turn into money-making ideas. Whilst the creation of the app will require very little technical knowledge, the resulting app may be difficult to transfer to an apps store to sell. However, free online apps creators are useful for testing out your apps. Free sites include www.android3apps.com for the Google Android operating system and www.createfreeiphoneapps.com for the iOS used by Apple devices (iPhone, iPad and iPod Touch).

Sell Your App

There are many ways to sell your apps, including dedicated apps stores, general apps websites and through your own website. Some of the poplar ones include the following:

Above: Free online apps creators such as ww.android3apps.com include a range of easy-to-create apps, from games and blogs to radio stations and e-books.

 Apple App Store: Apple has its own online apps store and charges 30% commission for the sale of an app. You decide the selling price and there are no fees for credit card payments, marketing and hosting. Payments for sales are made monthly.

 Amazon: Amazon's App Store currently supports apps created using the Android operating system and is only available in the USA. It charges a 30% commission on the selling price or 80% of the list price (whichever is greater). An annual developer program fee of $99 is also charged.

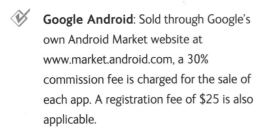 **Google Android**: Sold through Google's own Android Market website at www.market.android.com, a 30% commission fee is charged for the sale of each app. A registration fee of $25 is also applicable.

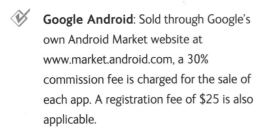 **Third-party apps stores**: There are numerous apps stores willing to sell your apps online. These include Getjar.com, Handango.com and Slideme.org.

Hot Tip

Find out how much you will be charged to sell your app through an online store. In some cases there is a commission fee, whereas others charge a registration fee.

Upload Your App

When you've chosen a particular online store to sell your app, you need to upload it. This involves registering with the app store (sometimes a registration fee is incurred), then completing some details concerning your app, such as a name for it, which language it uses, a description, category and price. Some stores have rules concerning minimum and maximum prices. Once an app has been uploaded, it usually needs to be approved before it's made available for purchasing.

Market Your App

Don't just rely upon an online apps store to sell your app. Several marketing techniques need to be adopted to ensure as many people as possible know about your app. This may involve selling your app through several online stores, creating publicity for it through social network sites and other websites, and advertising in magazines.

Above: Apps can be sold through a number of websites – www.appworld.blackberry.com sells a variety of apps created by different developers.

Other App Money Makers

Many apps include advertising to help generate income, where click-throughs and affiliate advertising techniques are used. The advertisements often appear at the beginning or end of the app. This works in a similar way to other forms of online advertising. However, some developers are also looking into product placement within their apps.

Surveys for Cash

Completing online surveys is a relatively straightforward method of making some money. Don't expect to become a millionaire from this, but in return for your opinions, you can build up a small sum of cash or discount vouchers. The following section explains what's involved in registering to complete surveys, how to complete them and what's generally involved in avoiding scams and trouble.

Above: Registering with online survey websites, such as www.toluna.com, often requires lots of personal information to help determine your suitability for particular surveys.

Preparation

Before you start signing up for surveys, a little preparation work is essential. Consider the following points:

 Email address: Surveys are usually emailed to you, so you may want to dedicate a particular email address to help monitor the flow of questionnaires and follow-up emails. This will help to see who has acquired your email address, especially if junk mail starts to flood in. It also helps to keep any personal email addresses separate and private.

 Find the surveys: Use Google, Yahoo! and other search engines to find a wide range of surveys that pay. Construct a list of them and compare what they offer. Some will offer payments in return for each survey, whilst others will award points, which can be exchanged for cash or vouchers with high street retailers.

Don't pay: If a survey website requests a registration or membership fee, do not pay. Most surveys should not require you to make a payment.

Survey Money Makers

There are various methods of making money from surveys. The most obvious is to complete a survey and be rewarded with a cash payment or points that build up to cash or a voucher to spend with a high-street retailer. However, there are often other incentives:

 Introductions: Introduce a friend to a survey website and, in some cases, you will also be rewarded.

 Competitions: Some surveys include a free entry to a competition alongside a payment. Small surveys, including mini-polls where payment is very small or non-existent, include competitions to tempt you.

 Cash prizes: Survey sites such as www.greatsites.co.uk offers cash prizes of up to £5000 for completing online surveys. The more surveys you complete, the greater the chance of winning the cash.

Revenue From Reviews

Review websites such as www.ciao.co.uk pay commission every time someone reads and rates your review of a product. Whilst the revenue only ranges from 0.5–2p per reader, the money can soon mount up if hundreds of thousands of people read it, especially if you are one of the first to write a review.

Online Finance

The internet can be used to monitor stocks and shares, bank accounts, pensions and other investments. It can also be used to look for the latest investment offers and switch money quickly to snap them up. The following section reveals what to look for how to avoid potential problems.

Above: Money Saving Expert's savings calculator helps to work out how much money you can make with a regular savings account. The website also lists the top savings accounts.

Financial Money Makers

There are manifold ways of making money from money, whether you are spending it or saving it. These include some of the following:

 Cashback credit cards: Some credit cards offer an annual percentage cashback (usually 0.5–3%) on purchases made, but always check the small print to see how long the offer lasts and whether there is an annual fee for the card.

 0% on purchases: Credit cards that offer 0% interest charges on purchases for several months are often lucrative if you can save the money to pay the credit card bill and either offset it against your mortgage or feed it into a high-interest savings account.

 Cash incentive bank accounts: Many banks and building societies offer cash payments to switch your accounts to them. Look out for any conditions, such as a minimum monthly salary or overdraft charges.

New account interest rates and bonuses: Look out for new account offers from banks and building societies with high interest rates and bonuses.

Managing Your Investments

Stocks and shares, pensions and bank and building society accounts can all be managed online, allowing you to move funds and buy and sell when you want. The internet is also a useful source of historical data, so you can see the past performance of shares, track interest rates and find out the exchange rate for a range of foreign currencies over several years.

Above: Historical exchange rate data is available at www.oanda.com, where you can compare two or more currencies over a few days or up to five years.

Security Issues

There are a number of potential problems regarding managing your finances online, which mainly concern fraud and theft. Potential problems include the following:

 Email scams: If you receive an email from one of your financial institutions claiming your account has been disabled due to a security threat and you need to click on a link within the email message to reactivate it, don't. This is a fraudulent email designed to capture your security details. Discard the email immediately.

 Hacking: Malicious programs and people may attempt to hack into your computer via the internet to obtain your security information concerning a bank account or similar account. Make sure you have an up-to-date virus checker with a firewall. Some financial institutions provide their own anti-hacking software, such as Rapport.

Online Gambling

The internet has a wide variety of online gambling websites, ranging from bingo and lottery tickets to poker and slot machines, but can you really make money from these activities? The following section outlines what they can offer and the problems that can arise.

Can You Really Make Money From Online Gambling?

This book does not recommend gambling as a means of making money from the internet, but the subject has been covered to help provide an overview and outline of the potential problems associated with this activity.

Types of Online Gambling

The main categories of online gambling are as follows:

- **Poker**: Tournaments are held between other online players. The website hosting the game takes a percentage of the money in the pot and often a tournament fee.

- **Casinos**: Just like a real casino with slot machines, roulette and black jack. Games are often played against the website.

- **Sports betting**: Most of the high-street bookmakers have an online betting website, allowing you to place bets on sporting events ranging from football to horse racing.

Bingo: Games are held online between several players. Free games are available with small prizes, but if you want a chance to win large sums of cash, you'll need to pay.

Lotteries: Most country's governments control their own lotteries, with websites dedicated to purchasing tickets online.

Mobile Gambling

The stigma of sitting in front of a computer late at night, indulging in online gambling has been marginally removed due to other means of accessing online gambling websites. Mobile devices, such as smartphones and tablets have enabled people to gamble in a more leisurely style. The mobile gambling market will undoubtedly be one of the most rapidly growing areas of the internet. In 2011, there were approximately 100 casino style mobile games (slot machines, video poker, bingo, blackjack, roulette) where you can play with real money.

Above: High-street bookmakers such as William Hill have catered for their customers via the internet, and just like many online gambling websites, provide offers to tempt newcomers.

Money Making Offers

Many online gambling websites try to tempt new customers with free cash to gamble with. This can be in the form of a free sum of money to start playing, or a percentage match for the money you put forward. Generally, this money cannot be withdrawn until several games have been played. With so many offers, you'd be right in thinking there is a formula to making money from online gambling, but don't forget about the websites that operate online gambling – they cannot afford to make a loss.

Gambling and the Law

There are different laws operating in a number of countries regarding the legalities of online gambling. Most countries have relaxed the rules, realizing there are tax advantages to this type of business; the USA has recently repealed the Unlawful Internet Gambling Enforcement Act of 2006, so people in the US can legally gamble online again. Other countries have a tighter control, such as Finland, where the government controls online casinos.

Above: Software such as Betfilter can be used to protect people from the risks of online gambling addiction.

Preventing Problems

Any form of gambling can lead to problems concerning addiction. If you plan to take part in online gambling, or want to avoid it, here are some useful points to consider:

 Protection: If you are concerned that other people who use your computer may use it for online gambling, install protection software such as Net Nanny to prevent these websites being accessed. Apps such as Betfilter.com can be used to block access to online gambling websites via a mobile device or a computer.

 Remove cookies: Once you've visited a number of online gambling websites, you may find the advertisements on other websites are all related to gambling. Delete the cookies in your internet browser and this will usually reduce these advertisements.

Making Money From Videos

Video hosting websites including YouTube have generated hundreds of millions of viewings for videos and turned amateur film makers into professionals. The following pages show what you need to do to be able to make money from hosting your own videos.

Video Money Makers

There are many methods, direct and indirect, of making money from creating your own video and hosting it through a website such as YouTube. These include the following:

- **Create a career**: Many artists, animators, film producers and musicians have used a video hosting website to promote their skills and gain commission for work.

- **Advertising**: Pop-up advertisements can be displayed near the bottom of a video whilst it's being played. Other links to advertising can also be added during the creation of the video.

- **Professional services**: If you offer a professional service, ranging from dressmaking to tuition, a video is a useful method of promotion, which can lead to new customers.

- **Selling a product**: Some video hosting websites will allow you to promote a product through a video. This can be done directly by reviewing the product and offering a link to purchase it, or providing an instruction video and displaying a link to your website where the product is sold.

 Video rentals: Video hosting websites such as YouTube offer a rental scheme where your video is streamed and viewers pay to watch it.

Success Story of a Watercolour Workshop

Left: Steven Cronin has uploaded instructional videos on painting to YouTube and used this to direct customers to buy his paintings on eBay and his DVDs on Amazon.

Artist Steven Cronin has produced and uploaded over 200 videos to YouTube (search for 'watercolour workshop') and received over one million viewings. The videos cover instructions on painting landscape scenes and include advertisements displayed along the bottom. However, Steven also sells his paintings via eBay and his videos in DVD format via Amazon. A link underneath his YouTube videos directs visitors to the DVDs he sells via Amazon and if you visit www.stevencronin.com, you'll be diverted to his eBay store where he sells watercolours.

Creating a Video

Internet broadcast quality videos can be created using a basic digital camera that can record video. Whilst this type of equipment is cheap and readily available, it helps to consider a few other issues to ensure your video looks as professional as possible, including the following:

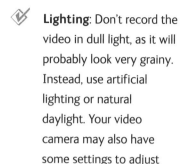

Lighting: Don't record the video in dull light, as it will probably look very grainy. Instead, use artificial lighting or natural daylight. Your video camera may also have some settings to adjust the lighting.

Background junk: Make sure you have a clean background when filming. Remove any unwanted clutter first.

Script: You may know what you want to say, but once the camera is recording, you'll be hesitating, thinking and saying 'erm' a lot, so write a brief script and practise it several times.

Record in chunks: Don't attempt to record a video in one take. Record several small parts, then use a video editor to put them together.

Adding Ads to Video

There are various ways to include advertisements within a video, depending on the type of revenue that can be gained from them. These include the following:

Product placement: If you are promoting a product within a video, whether it's a review or demonstration, this type of advertising can be used to link to websites where the product is sold.

✔ **Link ads**: Links to websites can be embedded into a video and clicked on to earn money from affiliate advertising and click-throughs.

✔ **Trailer ads**: Advertisements at the beginning of a video can be played with options to click on links. Many of these advertisements are often provided by professional hosting sites such as YouTube.

✔ **Running ads**: An advertisement can be displayed along the bottom of the video, which doesn't fully detract from viewing. This type of advertisement is popular with YouTube.

✔ **External ads**: Advertisements can be placed around the video, unless it is viewed in full-screen mode. These can be used to generate income in the form of affiliate advertising and click-throughs.

YouTube Eligibility

Not every video submitted to YouTube is eligible for advertising to make money. YouTube cannot include advertising with the following types of video:

✔ **Cover music**: If you produce a video of yourself playing or singing a song written by someone else, it cannot be supported with advertising unless you have the performance rights.

✔ **Other people's material**: Do not include video footage from films, television shows, live performances or other people's work unless you have permission and can prove this to YouTube.

✔ **Adult content**: YouTube does not host video that is of a sexually explicit nature, even if it is only of yourself. Similarly, it doesn't host videos showing violence or people being hurt.

Illegal activities: YouTube does not host video that shows illegal activities, such as drug taking, abusing animals or making bombs.

Beyond Advertising on YouTube

YouTube isn't just a useful resource for making money from advertisements linked to your uploaded videos. It can also be used to show your skills and generate work associated with your core business activities, ranging from recruiting staff to finding new customers.

Hot Tip

Create your own channel on YouTube to allow other YouTubers to subscribe and follow your work.

Success Story of Aniboom

The animation company Aniboom has used the internet including YouTube to attract both customers and staff. The company has been involved in major animation projects for worldwide clients including Fox, the History Channel, Sesame Street and Saatchi & Saatchi. Many people discover examples of the company's animation projects via YouTube where Aniboom has its own channel and a range of short animated videos. This method of marketing has helped to attract both new clients and animators and other people who are interested in working in this industry. Aniboom has also included advertisements with some of its YouTube animations, helping to generate additional income.

Above: Animation company Aniboom has used YouTube to host its own channel of animated video to help attract animators and customers.

Legal Issues

Avoiding Fraud

Making money and doing business over the internet have their fair share of problems. The following section deals with a wide range of risks, from email scams and hacking to credit card fraud and dishonest customers.

Scams

The vast assortment of scams on the internet range from tax refunds to offers to make you rich overnight. As a general rule, if it sounds too good to be true, it probably is, so be cautious with such offers. However, many of these scams are often not so obvious to identify. If you are selling goods via the internet, you may receive emails from suppliers, payment services and financial institutions that deal with your transactions or banking. In amongst all the legitimate communication you receive, scams can be difficult to recognize.

Common Scams

It can often be very difficult to identify a fraudulent or false email from a genuine one, as they frequently change and new ones emerge every week. Here are some of the most popular ones:

 False links: Never sign in to a bank, PayPal or other account via a link within an email. This is a common type of scam and often leads to a

> # Hot Tip
> **Invest in a reputable virus checker and firewall, and regularly run virus checks on your computer.**

fake website where your personal details are captured as you log in. Popular scams include security alerts, account suspended notifications and tax refunds.

 Payment made: Emails containing a receipt for goods purchased or a payment made, which you have not authorized are a common scam. Do not click on any links within the email, but check the account that has been supposedly debited.

Above: This supposed email from Microsoft is typical of a scam. It contains a link to capture personal information, but is easy to identify as fraudulent thanks to poor grammar and a non-Microsoft email address.

E-cards: Never download an e-card or click on a link to download a plug-in or other software to view a card. Even if the e-card is supposedly from someone you know, it may be a virus that has spread from their computer.

Funds transfer: Another common scam are the emails from someone who claims to have a large sum of money to transfer out of a country in trouble (Nigeria and Iraq are popular) and is looking for a bank account to transfer the money to. You are offered a large fee, but if you respond, you are told you have to first pay the transfer fees. These fees continue and you never see any money.

You won the lottery: Thousands of emails are produced claiming that you've won a lottery which you've never entered in a country you've never visited. In some cases, the prize money cannot be claimed until you've paid a fee, whereas in other cases, you have to submit personal details. In all cases, this is not a genuine lottery win.

Work from home: Emails claiming you can easily earn hundreds of pounds or dollars a day from very little work are often too good to be true. The sales pitch never reveals what the work involves, because it is often non-existent or a type of pyramid selling (illegal in many countries).

Data gathering: Some emails contain a program that can retrieve personal data from your computer. The program is often activated upon opening the email message.

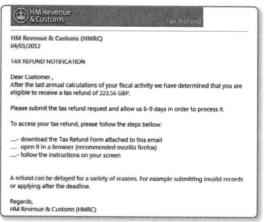

Right: This supposed email from the UK's tax office has an attachment designed to capture personal data. The tax refund sounds tempting and is one of the many persuasive approaches used by scams.

HM Revenue & Customs

HM Revenue & Customs (HMRC)
04/01/2012

TAX REFUND NOTIFICATION

Dear Customer,
After the last annual calculations of your fiscal activity we have determined that you are eligible to receive a tax refund of 223.56 GBP.

Please submit the tax refund request and allow us 6-9 days in order to process it.

To access your tax refund, please follow the steps bellow:

.....- download the Tax Refund Form attached to this email
..... open it in a browser (recommended mozilla firefox)
.....- follow the instructions on your screen

A refund can be delayed for a variety of reasons. For example submitting invalid records or applying after the deadline.

Regards,
HM Revenue & Customs (HMRC)

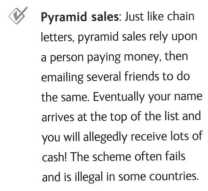 **Pyramid sales**: Just like chain letters, pyramid sales rely upon a person paying money, then emailing several friends to do the same. Eventually your name arrives at the top of the list and you will allegedly receive lots of cash! The scheme often fails and is illegal in some countries.

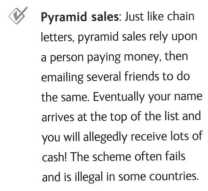 **Romance**: When someone you have never met is in love with you via email, don't believe a word of it.

Fraud on Fraud

The worst scams are those that prey on a person's vulnerability concerning their identity, reputation or money. The following scams are common via email and over the telephone:

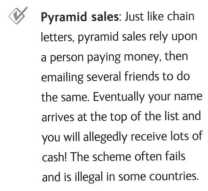 **ID theft prevention**: So called 'identity theft prevention services' have been known to contact people claiming to offer such services and request a person's personal details, which can then be used fraudulently.

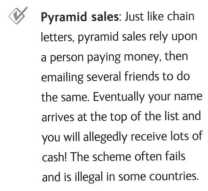 **Credit rating**: Companies claiming to improve a person's credit rating or remove a black listing that should not exist.

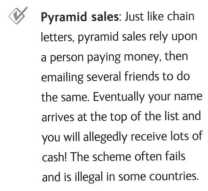 **Computer virus**: A popular money-making method is to telephone people and explain their computer has a virus, which can be removed if they pay a fee via a credit or debit card. This is usually a scam as the organization has no way of knowing whether a computer has a virus or not.

Card fraud: A telephone call is received explaining your credit or debit card has been used fraudulently, but before anything can be done about it, you need to run through some security questions. Whilst this may be genuine, do not reveal any details, hang up the phone and call the financial institution for the credit or debit card in question.

Non-scams Become Scams

Sometimes, a genuine idea to make money becomes a scam. For instance, Google cash was initially a legitimate business idea to create Google Ads and make money. There was even an e-book written on the subject by someone who claims to have made a lot of money from it. Sadly, there are many scammers who have taken this method of earning money and made it into a scam. Consequently, it's difficult to tell what is genuine and what is a waste of money. There are numerous training kits, books and videos promising to make you rich using Google Ads and other advertising techniques. Finding genuine material isn't always so easy.

Selling Trouble

The commonest problems that can arise with buying and selling over the internet include the following:

 Overpayment: If a payment is received via a cheque through the post and the amount is greater than the purchase price, do not provide an immediate refund for the difference until the cheque has cleared. This type of scam usually results in the cheque not clearing.

Goods not received: If you sell an item and deliver it, but the buyer claims it has not been received, you may have to provide a refund or send the same item again (if available). It often helps to use a traceable delivery service, even if the cost of delivery is more expensive.

 Used and returned: If a buyer returns a purchase, but when it comes back it has clearly been used, you may still have to offer a refund. This is a particular problem with goods that can be copied, such as an instruction booklet.

Business Scams

There is an ever-growing list of scams offering new business and investment opportunities and cheaper products that don't exist. Here are some of the most popular ones to avoid:

 Timeshare and travel: This involves discounted property share deals, plane tickets and tickets for major events that don't exist. If there is no means of getting a refund, don't become involved.

- **Government grants**: If your business is eligible for a grant, find out about it from the government body that awards it, not a third party that promises to process your application.

- **Fake suppliers**: Buying items from an unknown supplier to sell on can be risky. Many businesses use reputable and reliable wholesalers, but it's always tempting to use someone else, especially if they're cheaper. If you decide to use an unknown supplier, use PayPal or a similar service to hold the funds until the goods have been delivered and checked.

- **Ponzi and Madoff**: Investment schemes that offer returns from other people's money (also known as a pyramid scheme) are illegal in many countries. They use a chain letter method, but most people lose money. The scheme has been around since the nineteenth century. Well-known perpetrators include Charles Ponzi and Bernard Madoff.

- **Re-shipping**: Goods are ordered for an overseas delivery, but then the customer advises that the goods will be collected by an agent or freight representative. The customer orders an additional charge to be added to the total cost and for you to pay it to the person collecting the goods. You pay the collector, but never receive any payment.

Payment Fraud

Credit and debit card fraud is one of the biggest problems concerning trading on the internet. If you are receiving payments for goods via credit and debit cards, contact the organization managing these payments to find out what you need to do to avoid fraud. Also, find out whether there are any situations where you will lose money regardless of the precautions you take.

> **Hot Tip**
>
> eBay, Amazon and other selling websites provide ratings for buyers and sellers, so always check them out if you are concerned about doing business with someone.

Data Protection

If your business expands and builds up a list of clients, suppliers and other contacts, you need to make sure the information concerning these people and organizations is kept safe to avoid identity theft and fraud. In some countries, you have a legal obligation to store data securely.

Names and Addresses

The names and addresses of customers, suppliers and other business contacts should be stored securely to ensure they cannot be exploited by someone else. This would not only be bad news for them, but it could also damage your business. Make sure you have a suitable virus checker and firewall to help prevent the theft or misuse of these contact details. Ideally, the contact details should be stored in a database or similar file, which has a password to access it. In some countries you have a legal obligation to keep customers' details secure.

Newsletters

If you store customers' email addresses for newsletters, those addresses are personal information and should be safeguarded.

Payment Details

If you use a credit or debit card company or payment company such as PayPal, then you probably won't be able to store any details concerning customers' financial details. However, if you do store payment details, such as bank account or credit card details, then you must provide adequate security to ensure they cannot be stolen.

Quality Issues

If you sell goods that haven't passed safety tests in your country or the country you are selling to, or goods that have defects, you could be involved in a legal dispute. The following section outlines some of the problems that can arise and how they can be avoided.

Safety Checks

Some countries require a safety mark to be displayed on some goods. For instance, a piece of furniture may need to have a label proving its fire-proof qualities, a toy may need to have a safety code, and a product with glass may need to be fitted with safety glass. Before buying or acquiring such products to sell, check if any safety standards need to be adhered to. In some cases, such as electrical goods, you may be able to obtain a safety certificate for items.

Health Hazards

Some products are banned or illegal in particular countries, such as some face-bleaching products. Whilst you may find a cheap product in a particular country that can be sold in your home country, check that it does not contain banned substances or that the product itself is not banned.

Faulty Goods

Goods that are faulty will need to be returned, especially if they are discovered to be faulty after they have been sold. However, if the goods are dangerous because they are faulty, you may have a legal obligation as a seller to have tested or checked them, especially if you are the agent for them in your country.

Recalls

If a product is recalled because it is defective, you may have to contact all of your customers who have bought it and arrange for their purchases to be returned. If the supplier of your products doesn't offer any assistance with recalls, you may find you are incurring unwanted expenses.

Hot Tip

If any goods you are buying have serial numbers, find out if you can use them to check whether they have been stolen.

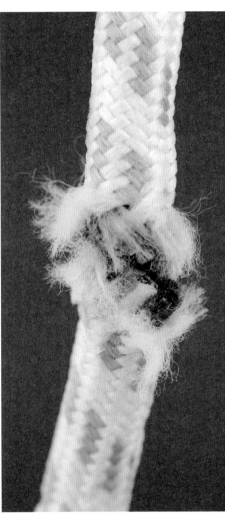

Stolen Goods

Selling stolen goods is one of the biggest problems associated with selling. Most traders want to deal with reputable wholesalers and other suppliers. However, if you source some goods and discover they have been stolen, you may be required by law to hand them over to the police.

Copyright

The content of your website and anything you advertise through selling sites must not be copied from other sources unless you have permission. If you are involved in illegally sharing music and other files, this can lead to court action or extradition to another country.

Get Permission

If you intend to use an image that has been produced by someone else on a website or when selling an item, make sure you have permission to do so. You may need to include a credit to the owner of the image.

Hot Tip

Don't copy other people's ads through eBay and use them as your own. You will risk being reported, having your listing removed and, at worst, being banned.

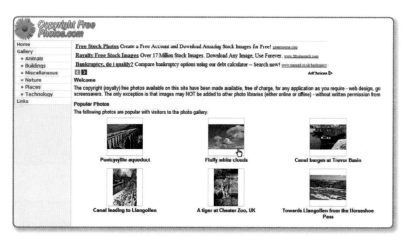

Above: Free images are available from websites including www.copyrightfreephotos.com, which helps to avoid any potential legal disputes.

Existing Permission

Selling websites such as eBay have a large stock of product images. These can be used to sell items, but cannot be copied and used on other websites. However, there is a large stock of free-to-use images, which was outlined in chapter five (Make a Website).

Avoid Confrontation

Whether you are legally allowed to use someone else's image on a website or not, it is sometimes best to contact them and gain permission rather than becoming involved in a legal battle and unnecessary expenses. Third-party legal teams can see their commission building up when someone unlawfully uses an image, allowing them to think up a fee and add a few noughts on the end of it.

Business Name

If you are launching a new business with a new name, you may want to look into whether this name has already been used and if you are allowed to use it. Even if you only want to use part of the name of a business, this may result in problems.

Domain Names

When deciding to trade under a business name, make sure it hasn't been used before and see if you can find a suitable domain name that is available. Choosing a domain name was covered in depth in chapter five, with information on how to look for a domain name and register it.

XXX Trouble

In 2010, domain names ending with .xxx were introduced in a bid to clearly separate the adult entertainment market. However, you may find you want to purchase

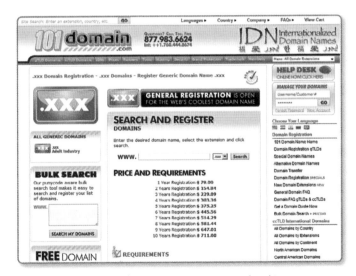

Above: Domain names with an xxx extension were introduced in an attempt to separate the adult entertainment market from the rest of the internet. Domain name providers such as www.101domain.com can acquire these extensions.

this version for your own domain name to avoid any potential confusion with an explicit site that may use this extension with the same domain name as you.

Lawsuits from Overseas

There have been a number of legal cases concerning the illegal sharing of files, confidential data and displaying sources where files can be obtained. These cases have often originated overseas and have resulted in successful financial settlements or even extradition requests. Whilst you can make sure the content on your own website is legal, problems can arise if you are recommending other websites that contain illegal content.

Music File Sharing

Websites that host illegal music files have resulted in successful legal action both against the websites and the people who use them. In some cases, visitors to the website have downloaded music files, resulting in their own computers being used as a server to share files.

This has resulted in a greater degree of illegal action beyond obtaining files. If you are unsure about the content provided by a website, do not recommend it or become involved in any form of advertising with it, especially if it will earn money for you.

UK Student Faces Extradition Over TV Shack

Richard O'Dwyer of the UK faced extradition to the USA in 2012 following claims he set up a website called TV Shack that provided links to films and TV shows that could be watched for free. Whilst not illegal in the UK, it is in the USA and Richard faced charges of copyright infringement and conspiracy to infringe copyright. According to the US authorities, advertising incorporated in the TV Shack website has generated income in excess of $230,000 (£147,000) since January 2008.

Check Your Links

Make sure any links contained within your website lead to websites that have legal content. This can be difficult in some instances, such as where you are recommending free downloads. Even if the content is not illegal in your own country, it may mean legal action can be taken against you in another country. Where money is involved, such as advertising revenue or the sale of downloads, the severity of the crime is magnified. So if you are at all unsure about a link to specific content, do not include it.

Paying Tax

When does a hobby that makes money turn into a business that needs to be registered and paying tax? The following section provides the guidance you may need to ensure you don't get stung with an unwanted tax bill.

Tax Laws

The laws of taxation differ between countries, so it's impossible to comment on each one, especially considering taxation usually changes each year. However, there are some general considerations, which should be taken into account if you start making money on the internet. These include the following:

 Personal goods: If you are selling items that you once owned, then most countries do not require you to declare this activity as a business and so you don't have to pay tax.

Personal limits: Some countries have a limit on the number of specific items that can be sold before you have to declare yourself as a business. In the UK, for instance, if you sell more than six motor vehicles in a 12-month period, you are classed as a dealer.

Buying and selling: If you buy goods to sell on for a profit, in most countries you need to register your business with the tax office and start keeping records.

> ## Hot Tip
> **If you are concerned about tax in the UK, visit www.taxaid.org.uk.**

Selling for others: If you are selling items for other people and earning a commission from each sale, then this activity should be registered as a business.

Business Benefits

Registering a business with the tax office doesn't always result in a hefty tax bill. If your internet-based business is part-time and funded by a full-time job, you may find it makes a loss at first, which in some countries entitles you to a tax refund from the tax paid on your full-time job. In most countries, the expenses incurred in running a business are deducted from the turnover to derive the net profit, which in turn determines the amount of tax to pay. These expenses vary from country to country, but generally they can include the following:

 Goods purchased: The cost of goods bought to be sold has to be deducted in some way, but in some cases is reflected in any stock held.

Direct expenses: Costs incurred in the course of your business activities, such as postage of goods, packaging, delivery and any manufacturing can be claimed.

Operating costs: These cover anything that enables you to run your business, ranging from the use of a telephone line and hosting costs for a website to renting storage space or using a delivery van.

Introducing equipment: Some tax rules allow you to value and introduce equipment to a business, such as a computer to access your website, a camera to photograph goods you are selling, an old filing cabinet for paperwork and a desk and chair.

New equipment: When new equipment is purchased, such as a computer, this is treated as a type of cost and accounted for straight away or depreciated over a number of years.

Personal use: The cost of some items may need to be divided up between personal and business use, so only a fraction of the expenses are claimed. For example, if you use the family car half of the time for business trips, then only half the car's costs can be accounted for as an expense.

Use of home: If you operate your internet business from home, then you can either allocate a percentage of bills (electricity, gas and telephone) for business use or in some countries, allocate a charge for using a room in the house for business purposes. The same may apply if you use the garage for storage.

Preventative Action on eBay

You can avoid some problems before they occur, such as buyers who don't pay for listings on eBay and sellers who steal your images. The following section outlines some of the problems that can arise and how eBay can help to avoid or smooth over them.

Buyers That Don't Pay on eBay

When someone wins an auction for an item you are selling, or clicks on the 'Buy it now' button but doesn't pay or collect the goods, what can you do? eBay has a number of solutions to help sort out such a problem or prevent it happening again in the future.

Insist on PayPal

By insisting that the purchase of a listing is made via PayPal, this ensures you receive the money from the buyer. If you are selling an expensive item that needs to be collected, insist a deposit is paid via PayPal within a given number of days and either cash is brought by the buyer or the outstanding amount is paid before collection.

Above: Many eBay listings with a 'Buy it now' feature can include a commit-to-buy option where the buyer has to pay through PayPal or another secure means to purchase the item.

Check Ratings

If you are unsure about a buyer and whether they will pay, either check their ratings or state in your listing that anyone with a feedback rating under a specific value must contact you first.

Use Unpaid Item Assistant

eBay's Unpaid Item Assistant can be used to resolve disputes where a buyer has not paid. It can also be used to help protect future listings. Providing a listing can be paid for using PayPal or a similar electronic method, the following instructions explain how to set up eBay's Unpaid Item Assistant to send automatic reminders to the buyer if payment is not received.

 Log in: Open eBay via your web browser, log in and click on 'My eBay' from the menu near the top of the screen, then select 'Summary'. Select the 'Account' tab near the top of the screen, then click on 'Site preferences' in the list on the left side of the screen.

Above: If you are having trouble with buyers not paying, then eBay's Unpaid Item Assistant can help. It is found under the 'Summary' section of 'My eBay'. Click on the 'Account' tab and select 'Site preferences'.

 Open Unpaid Item Assistant: Scroll down the screen and look for 'Unpaid Item Assistant', which is listed under the first category – 'Selling preferences'. Click on the 'Show' option to the far right of the Unpaid Item Assistant. The words 'Hide' and 'Edit' will appear – click on 'Edit'. The screen will change to reveal several settings for the Unpaid Item Assistant.

Check case days: Select the option labelled 'Yes – I want Unpaid Item Assistant to open and close cases on my behalf'. Further options will appear, allowing you to change the settings for the Unpaid Item Assistant. Check how many days are specified before eBay will open a case if a payment isn't received. This can be changed, but if it can't, select 'Click here' to change the number of days allowing buyers to make combined payments.

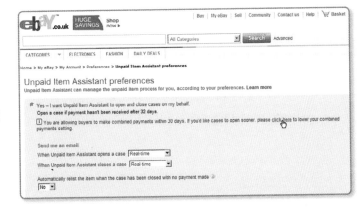

Above: If the Unpaid Item Assistant preferences screen does not allow you to change the number of days set before opening a case (displayed as 32 here), select 'click here.'

 Change combined payment dates: Under the 'Combined payments' section, click on 'Edit' to change the number of days within which a buyer can make a single payment for items purchased. A second

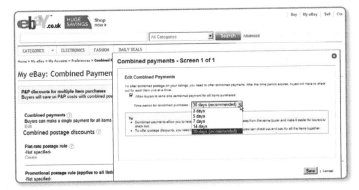

Above: By changing the number of days for a combined payment, you can then change the number of days before a case is opened for an unpaid listing.

smaller window will appear on screen. Choose the number of days within which a payment can be made for combined purchases, then save and return to the Unpaid Item Assistant preferences. After changing this setting, it usually activates the setting for opening a case if a payment hasn't been received!

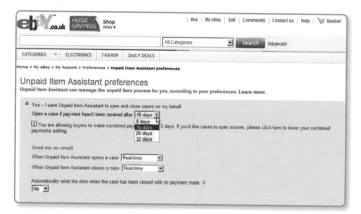

 Exclude good payers: If you have a number of reliable customers that usually pay for their purchases on time, you may want to exclude them from the Unpaid Item Assistant. Under the preferences section, you can add their user IDs as a list (separate each one with a comma, space, new line or semi-colon).

 Automatic relist: If a listing isn't paid for and eBay doesn't manage to resolve this problem by opening a case, then eBay can automatically relist the item for you. This option is listed under the Unpaid Item Assistant preferences screen.

In some cases, eBay will automatically provide a credit for the final value fee that was incurred and you may also receive a refund' for the insertion fee.

Protect Your Listings

One of the biggest problems with creating a listing on eBay is that someone else copies and uses it. This is especially frustrating if you've spent a lot of time taking photographs and writing interesting and informative text. There are, however, a number of solutions to help prevent your listings being copied.

Personalize Text

Write your text from a personal angle and include details that cannot apply to anyone else. For example, if you are selling a second-hand item, mention the length of time you have owned it, what you have used it for and any other personal information. Write the text in a graphics program, then save it as an image. Insert the image into your eBay listing and although the image can be copied, the text within it cannot be altered.

Hot Tip

Display your website address across an image to prevent it being copied.

Watermark Photographs

Some image editing programs can add a watermark across a photograph, which allows you to reduce the risk of other people copying and using your images. Some professional programs, such as Photoshop CS, allow a digital watermark to be added to an image, which further restricts the use and editing of an image. This can also be useful for images displayed on your website.

Above: Adding a digital watermark to an image can help reduce the risk of it being copied. This can be completed using software such as Photoshop CS.

Further Reading

Buddy, Johnline, *The Beginner's Guide to Making Money on the Internet with Micro Niches*, Kindle Edition, 2012

Burns-Millyard, Kathy, *Turning Your Computer Into a Cash Cow... A Reality Check about Making Money Online*, Electronic Perceptions, 2011

Collier, Marsha; Hill, Steve., Hoskyn, Jane., *eBay.co.uk for Dummies*, For Dummies, 2011

Cooper, Douglas, *Beginners Guide to Making Money on the Internet*, Kindle Edition, 2011

Craypoe, Bob, *All About the Numbers: The Truth About Making Money on the Internet*, Craypoe Publications, 2010

Devonshire, Mario, *Making Money Online as a YouTube Partner*, Paper Mind Publishing, 2012

Fox, Scott C., *Internet Riches. The Simple Money-Making Secrets of Online Millionaires*, Amacom, 2006

Granai, Gary, *Internet Business Planning – Simple Ways to Make Money on the Internet*, Small Business Academy, 2011

Human, King, *Million Dollar Goldmine: Making Money on the Internet*, Kindle Edition, 2011

Jordaan, Petrus, *Ways to Start Your Own Online Business, Advertise and Make Money on the Internet*, Kindle Edition, 2011

McFall, Brett, *How to Make Money While You Sleep: How to Start, Promote and Profit from an Online Business*, Wrightbooks, 2008

Omoregie, E.M., *Internet Goldmines: A Practical Guide to Making Money on the Internet*, Omoregie Publishing, 2005

Ostrofsky, Marc, *Get Rich Click!: The Ultimate Guide to Making Money on the Internet*, Simon & Schuster Ltd, 2012

Pugh, Robert, *The eBay Business Handbook, 3rd Edition: How Anyone Can Build a Business and Make Big Money on eBay.co.uk*, Harriman House Publishing, 2010

Tiong, M.H., *3 Most Popular Ways of Making Money on the Internet*, Kindle Edition, 2012

VanBergen, David, *How to Make Money Online: A Step by Step Guide to Making Money on the Internet*, CreateSpace, 2011

Vitale, Joe; Wheeler, Jillian Coleman, *Your Internet Cash Machine: The Insiders' Guide to Making Big Money, Fast!*, John Wiley & Sons Ltd, 2008

Webster, Blake; Boga, Steve, *Make-Money-Online Series: How to Make Money Writing for the Internet: A Step-by-Step Guide to Publishing Your Work Online*, CreateSpace, 2011

Wilson, Dan, *Make Serious Money on eBay UK: Build a successful business online and profit from eBay, Amazon and your own website* (2nd revised Edition), Nicholas Brealey Publishing, 2009

Websites

www.youtube.com/partners
YouTube's help pages covering making money from uploading your own videos.

www.shuntmoney.co.uk
How to make money from writing online material, including using revenue sharing and social media websites.

www.copyblogger.com/write-and-sell-ebook
How to write an e-book and make money from it.

www.e-bookdirectory.com/howto.shtml
Information on writing e-books and how to publish them.

www.powersellerpod.com
Amanda O'Brien's website covering advice and information on selling through eBay and how to use effective selling methods.

www.easyprofits.co.uk
How to make money from eBay and other online money-making methods.

www.problogger.net/make-money-blogging
Pro Blogger's web pages covering advice on how to make money from blogging, including affiliate programs, e-books, continuity programs and speaking fees.

http://christianpf.com/how-to-make-money-with-a-blog
Personal account of how blogging generates extra income. Part of the Christian Personal Finance website, which provides money-related information.

www.make-a-web-site.com
Tom Jones' straightforward guide to creating your own website.

www.electroniccommerce101.com
Free online guide to getting started in e-commerce, with information on planning, creating a website, selling and the technicalities of online sales.

Index